BUSINESS

COMMUNICATIONS

INTERNATIONAL CASE
STUDIES IN ENGLISH

ENGLISH FOR SPECIFIC PURPOSES SERIES

Ann Johns, San Diego State University
Series Editor

Business Communications: International Case Studies in English
Drew Rodgers, Norwegian School of Management

BUSINESS

COMMUNICATIONS

INTERNATIONAL CASE
STUDIES IN ENGLISH

Drew Rodgers

Norwegian School of Management

St. Martin's Press
New York

Editor: Naomi Silverman
Managing editor: Patricia Mansfield Phelan
Project editors: Erica Appel, Melissa Holcombe
Production supervisor: Joe Ford
Art director: Sheree Goodman
Text and cover design: Christine Gehring Wolf
Photo research: Inge King
Cover photo: New York Stock Exchange, © 1991 David McGlynn, FPG International Corp.

Acknowledgment

The financial statements in "Larry the Liquidator vs. New England Wire and Cable," the organizational charts in "Commutair," and the case "Smith Brothers and Florida Central" are reprinted by permission of Grace Murphy.

Photo credits

p. 3: Frank Siteman/Stock, Boston
p. 12: Peter Menzel/Stock, Boston
p. 22: Spencer Grant/The Picture Cube
p. 33: Spencer Grant/Monkmeyer
p. 43: Mitch Wojnarowicz/The Image Works
p. 51: Rob Crandal/The Image Works
p. 60: Mike Kagan/Monkmeyer
p. 68: Nancy Bates/The Picture Cube
p. 78: Bob Kramer/The Picture Cube
p. 88: Richard Pasley/Stock, Boston
p. 97: Mimi Forsyth/Monkmeyer
p. 102: Stephen Agricola/Stock, Boston
p. 108: Cameramann/The Image Works
p. 116: Courtesy of Saturn Corporation

To Inger

PREFACE

AUDIENCE

Business Communications: International Case Studies in English is intended for use in ESP-Business for advanced-intermediate to advanced students. The case study approach allows for the teaching of both language and communication skills by actively engaging the students in the solution of realistic business cases, thus requiring the constant use and development of these skills. The students are required to bring their knowledge of business to bear on the cases; thus, a business background is *not* a requirement to teach this course, as your students will be encouraged to share their knowledge to create the atmosphere of cooperation fundamental to this approach. Those cases which require the least amount of business background are

Case 1: Preparing for Your Future

Case 4: Long-range Golf Equipment Seeks a Distributor

Case 5: Midland Heating and Cooling vs. the Primary Sheet Metal Workers of America, AFL-CIO

Case 6: Northern Electrical Services vs. the Environmentalists

Case 7: Commutair: Employee Motivation and Management Theory

Case 8: Unhealthy Leaders: Sterling Forklift

THE CASE STUDY METHOD AND ITS APPLICATION

The case study method is based on the approach used in programs at Harvard Business School and other major schools of business. The cases in this book have been developed to teach ESP. This approach is better adapted to teaching ESP-Business than the traditional teacher-centered approach because it develops communicative competence by putting the students in the center of the action, where they can use language actively and practice communication skills.

The role of the teacher becomes that of facilitator, reference person, and provider of feedback, and *the classroom becomes a workshop in communication and language skill development*. After the cases are introduced, much of the class time is spent in group work in which the students prepare their roles.

The teacher aids this preparation by providing language input. The students will often ask for vocabulary and structures, which they will use immediately and thus internalize better than in rote memorization. The facilitator role helps create a *dynamic partnership* in learning between the teacher and students, thus greatly enhancing the learning experience. In the *active approach to learning* fostered by this method, the students will achieve *communicative competence* in English more efficiently.

Think about the traditional teacher-centered method, in which the instructor is the hub and all communication goes through him or her. Learning a language and communication skills requires active participation. If only one student can speak at a time, how much learning can be accomplished? With the case study method, on the other hand, students are allowed to communicate in their individual groups, thereby multiplying the opportunities to produce language and to be corrected, as well as to practice communication skills.

This method allows the students to expand their repertoire of communication skills by requiring them to develop presentation, teamworking, and networking skills, as well as critical/analytical problem-solving skills, all of which are required in a modern business context characterized by a task force or team approach.

This method does not exclude teacher-centered activities. Rather, such activities are integrated through the processes of defining and clarifying the cases or working on grammar and vocabulary. However, once these tasks are completed, the students should be allowed to communicate more freely.

If you have no previous experience in the case study method, rest assured that it is one of the easiest methods to use, once the proper mind-set is adopted. Such a mind-set requires ceding center stage to the students and assuming a support role. Instead of leading the class, the teacher's role is to focus on providing the students with vocabulary, grammatical structures, and content feedback.

OVERVIEW AND ORGANIZATION

Business Communications is divided into cases representing various fields of business, such as finance, marketing, business organization and management, and human resource management. The cases are arranged in a pedagogical order, which is explained in the Instructor's Manual.

The cases are divided into two major groups: closed-ended and open-ended. The closed-ended cases are at the beginning of the book (Case 1 to Case 9). All information needed to solve these cases is presented in the cases themselves (with the exception of Case 1: Preparing for Your Future, which requires some knowledge of local companies). The open-ended cases are a unique feature of this book as they are set in the students' local environment in order to encourage them to develop information-gathering skills and to apply their knowledge in real-life situations. If the class setting is Germany, for example, the students can look into local German conditions to solve the cases. If the class is held in an English-speaking country, the students can look into those local conditions to get a better picture of the business culture of that country.

Each case consists of

1. A cultural background section to explain cultural factors bearing on the case, which may be unfamiliar to non-native students
2. A description of the situation underlying the case
3. Discussion questions to help the student consider general aspects of the case
4. The case activity and roles to be played
5. Language mastery exercises to help prepare for the case
6. Written exercises as a follow-up to the case activity
7. Vocabulary and other support materials

Each case is a complete unit and is pedagogically segmented to provide a logical progression in the solving of the case.

In addition to the cases, three appendices are included:

Appendix 1: Telephone English is designed to help students develop telephone-related skills and language as well as accepted telephone etiquette.

Appendix 2: Business Writing provides models for letters, reports, and memos, as well as discussions of (a) proper tone and style and (b) audience-centered communication, to aid students in completing the written assignments in each case.

Appendix 3: Electronic Communication Devices provides a brief description of E-mail and electronic bulletin boards.

An Instructor's Manual accompanies this text. It provides an in-depth explanation of the rationale behind the case study method, the teacher's and students' roles, the progression from introduction to writing assignment in the cases, and tips relevant to teaching each individual case. Thus, no previous experience with the case study method is necessary to use this book successfully.

ACKNOWLEDGMENTS

All the cases have been reviewed by experts in their respective fields, as well as by professionals in the field of education. I wish to thank the following members of the College of Business and the Labor Research Center at the University of Rhode Island for their suggestions: Dr. Kapil Jain, Dr. Chai Kim, Dr. Laura Beauvais, and Dr. Charles Schmidt. Thanks also to Grace Murphy, who served as my research assistant and provided necessary accounting documents and organization charts for the cases. A special thanks to Dr. Barbara Tate for a general review and to my editor, Naomi Silverman. Every author should be fortunate enough to have an editor like her. Finally, thanks to the reviewers who provided insightful suggestions that were incorporated into this book: Patricia Byrd, Georgia State University; Susana Christie, San Diego State University; Charles Cooper, Norwegian School of

Management; Lizabeth England, Eastern Michigan University; William H. Oliver, Evergreen State College; Miguel Parmantie, Universidad Pontificia Comillas (Madrid, Spain); Philip Vassallo, Middlesex County College; Kay Westerfield, University of Oregon; and Peter Cleaverley, Norwegian School of Management.

Drew Rodgers

CONTENTS

CASE 8 BUSINESS ORGANIZATION AND MANAGEMENT
Unhealthy Leaders: Sterling Forklift   68

Cultural Background: Anglo/American Management Styles   69

CASE 9 BANKING
Smith Brothers and Florida Central   78

Cultural Background: Loan Applications   79

Introduction to Open-Ended Cases

BUSINESS

COMMUNICATIONS

INTERNATIONAL CASE
STUDIES IN ENGLISH

INTRODUCTION

TO THE STUDENT

You are the key to the success of the teaching method behind this book.

You will be the focus of this method because it depends on your ability to play the roles assigned to you. You must actively share your knowledge of business in solving the cases. *You are the experts*. The more you share your knowledge, the better the class will be.

Although this book is designed for ESP-Business courses, the method will allow you to learn more than just English. You will learn many skills that are valuable in the business world, including:

1. How to make public presentations
2. How to actively share your knowledge of the business world so as to improve your marketability as a candidate for future jobs (a process known as *networking*)
3. How to work in teams
4. How to find necessary information
5. How to deal with foreign cultures, their values and ways of doing business
6. How to actively participate in problem-solving activities

However, in order to learn these skills, you will have to follow three basic rules:

1. *Be active* in all group and class work. You have to participate to learn.
2. *Speak only English* in class, except when you do not know a word and need to ask a fellow student or the instructor for a translation.
3. *Come to class prepared*. Remember, the role-playing on which this method is based depends on your preparedness and ability to play the roles assigned to you.

If you follow these three basic rules, you will not only learn English, you will also develop the six skills listed above, thereby greatly improving your chances in a competitive job market.

Some of the cases are set in an Anglo/American context, and all of them reflect certain Anglo/American values. Thus, a cultural background section is included to help you understand each case's cultural context. A language is a product of the culture of the people who speak it. Thus, both the cultural background

1

sections and the solving of the cases will help you gain a better understanding of Anglo/American culture.

There are no right answers. Each group will have to work out its own solutions and present them in the role-playing. You will all be expected to solve problems, use your communication skills to present your solutions, and help each other by sharing your ideas. This approach is not only an excellent way to learn language and communication skills — it is also fun. Good luck.

TO THE INSTRUCTOR

The level of this book is advanced-intermediate to advanced. It is intended for businesspeople and students of business in both non–English-speaking countries and schools of business in English-speaking countries. The accompanying Instructor's Manual provides an introduction to teaching with the case study method, detailed information on how to teach each case, advice on teaching vocabulary and grammar, the teaching sequence for each case (that is, how much time to devote to each part of the case), and secret position papers for the negotiation cases.

OVERVIEW OF CASE LEVELS

Case 1: Preparing for Your Future — advanced-intermediate

Case 2: Portfolio Development — advanced-intermediate

Case 3: Larry the Liquidator vs. New England Wire and Cable — advanced-intermediate

Case 4: Long-range Golf Equipment Seeks a Distributor — advanced-intermediate

Case 5: Midland Heating and Cooling vs. the Primary Sheet Metal Workers of America, AFL-CIO — advanced-intermediate

Case 6: Northern Electrical Services vs. the Environmentalists — advanced-intermediate

Case 7: Commutair: Employee Motivation and Management Theory — advanced-intermediate

Case 8: Unhealthy Leaders: Sterling Forklift — advanced-intermediate

Case 9: Smith Brothers and Florida Central — advanced

Case 10: Penetrating the Market with Long-range Clubs and Bags — advanced-intermediate

Case 11: Costa de los Años de Oro — advanced-intermediate

Case 12: Industrial Pollution: Charting Pollution and Proposing Solutions — advanced-intermediate

Case 13: Competing Internationally — advanced

Case 14: Saturn: Can American Automobile Manufacturers Compete with the Japanese — advanced

1

JOB SEARCH

Preparing for Your Future

CULTURAL BACKGROUND: JOB INTERVIEWS

Applicants for jobs in Anglo/American cultures are expected to sell themselves. They must show what they have accomplished and convince the interviewer that they will benefit the company. They should speak of their accomplishments and what they can contribute to the company, and they should be prepared to emphasize their strong points. To people from certain cultures, this may seem like bragging. In some cultures, employment is based on one's papers, and interviews are not even held. However, Anglo/American cultures emphasize the individual, seeking candidates with traits such as the ability to cooperate, communicate, and work in teams. Thus, the personal interview is important, and the personal impression a candidate makes may be as important as his or her educational background and work experience. Thus, the tendency in certain cultures to be modest and to understate one's qualifications may be a disadvantage. Instead, one must express self-confidence, and this is done by expressing one's accomplishments. In addition, direct eye contact, which may be considered impolite in certain cultures, is expected in an Anglo/American interview situation. In order to prepare for such interviews, candidates should do a personal inventory, discovering what educational background and work experience they have that are relevant to the job. Then they should express it in a practice interview before the real one.

CASE

With increasing competition in the job market, any new graduate who hopes to get a job should have a plan worked out long before graduation day. The purpose of this case is to help you begin to develop such a plan. One important step is to recall and share past work-related experiences with one another (remember that one of the skills you wish to develop is *networking* — the sharing of information that can benefit all members of the group). The résumé and cover letter you write in this case will present you as the candidate you want to be by the time you graduate. In preparing this résumé and cover letter, then, you will be shaping goals to aim for in becoming this ideal candidate. This case will not only take you through the steps involved in getting a job, it will also give you tips on how to succeed in your job search.

Start Preparing Now

What can you do now to ease the transition from student to professional? There are numerous ways to get your foot in the door (that is, to establish contacts with potential future employers) before you actually start looking for work. The more employers who know you before you start applying for a job, the greater your chance of being hired. Here are some tips that you can use to prepare yourself in advance.

1. Start files on companies you are interested in, so that you are well informed about the companies that may eventually be interviewing you.

2. Read professional journals, the business sections of newspapers, and business magazines. This will give you an idea of available jobs and the kind of education and experience they require. It will also help you tailor your courses and your experience to make you a competitive candidate.

3. Join clubs on campus that are related to your areas of interest, and invite potential future employers to speak to club members. Take advantage of the opportunity to establish personal contact with the speakers when they come to speak.

4. Connect your school projects with potential employers so that those employers can see you in action. If you do a good job, they will find you a more interesting candidate than someone they have never seen.

5. Informational interviews can also help you get a foot in the door. For example, in order to write an article for the school newspaper, you might interview directors of personnel about the present job market: expected trends, what they are looking for in a new graduate, what specialties are in demand, and so on. When you complete your article, send a copy of it with a note of thanks to the person you interviewed. You could use your studying of this case as a reason for arranging an informational interview.

6. Talk to friends working in your field of interest to find out what is happening in the job market. Let people know in advance that you will be looking for a job in the fall or spring of 19——.

POINTS FOR DISCUSSION

1. Discuss job-finding strategies.
2. Brainstorm on techniques for getting your foot in the door.
3. Discuss the do's and don'ts of applying and interviewing.
4. Discuss ways in which the job application process in your country is different from the one described in this case.

CASE ACTIVITIES

Interview Preparation and Interviewing

Each group should begin by finding an advertisement in a newspaper or journal for a job that the group members are interested in, then doing some research on the company. If you cannot find an appropriate job in the newspaper, create a job description and write an announcement for a job within an actual company. If group members have such different backgrounds that, realistically, they would not all apply for the same job, create several different job descriptions, all within the same company. Each group member will be interviewed by the other group members. Thus, you will each play the role of both applicant and interviewer. The interview situation will rotate as group member A will be interviewed by the group members B, C, and D, then group member B will be interviewed by group members A, C, and D, and so on. Thus, all group members must know something about the company in order to ask intelligent questions as interviewers and to answer them as candidates. After all the candidates have been interviewed, each group will present to the class the candidate who obtained the job, explaining why this candidate was chosen and the others were not.

Preparation

You will prepare just as if you were actually applying for the job. You will write a cover letter and a résumé (see Figure 1-1), and you will research the company. The best sources of information are annual reports and articles in newspapers and business journals. You want to have enough information so that you can answer questions intelligently and show that you know something about the company. The more you know about the company, the more you can present yourself as the candidate they are seeking.

     You should have a friend give you a trial interview, using the standard questions below. The goal is not to have "canned" answers (answers that you memorize and repeat word for word) to all questions, but to have the chance to think through what you really believe and feel and to develop experience in interviewing so that you will feel confident when the actual interview occurs. You should have a ninety-second answer to the question, "Tell me about yourself." It is important that you give concrete examples. Don't just say that you are a hard worker. Give examples from your education or work experience or references.

Standard Questions Asked during Interviews

These questions can be used during the trial interview, along with questions specific to the job and the individual candidate based on that person's résumé. Practice answering these questions in pairs prior to your trial interview.

1. Tell me about yourself (your background).
2. How would you describe yourself (your personality)?
3. What would you consider your greatest strengths and weaknesses?
4. What two or three accomplishments have given you greatest satisfaction?
5. How did you choose the career you have chosen, and what have you done to prepare for it?
6. What qualifications do you have to help you succeed in this career?
7. Why did you apply for a job with our company?
8. What do you think it takes to be successful in our company?

Joseph Daniels
2321 Park Drive
Providence, RI 02908
(401) 831-2365

Career Objective:	A sales position in an international company where I can use my knowledge of languages and foreign cultures.
Education:	University of Rhode Island, B.A., 1995 Marketing/Spanish • 3.25 GPA overall; 3.5 Marketing; 3.7 Spanish • Dean's List, four semesters • Relevant Courses: International Marketing Marketing and the Media Business Spanish The Business Culture of Latin America
Work Experience:	*Graduation Rings, Inc.,* 1993–present • Marketed and sold rings, pins, and accessories on campus. Increased sales at GRI by 25 percent. • Allowed me the opportunity to design and test marketing strategies. *Promotions, Inc.,* Summers, 1992–1994 • Layout, paste-up, and camera. Gave me insight into designing and visual presentation of advertisements.
Organizations:	American Marketing Association, President, 1994–1995 • Arranged the career day and a guest lecture series for marketing students.
Special skills:	Layout, paste-up, and camera Fluent in Spanish FORTRAN, Basic, Desktop Publishing

Figure 1-1 Sample Résumé

9. Where do you see yourself in five years?

10. Why should I hire you?

11. How do you work under pressure? Give me some examples.

12. Are you willing to relocate?

13. What are the three most important things to you in a job?

LANGUAGE MASTERY EXERCISE

Using Power Verbs

Use power verbs (verbs that create a strong impression of action) such as the following:

achieved	expanded	maintained	saved
administered	formulated	managed	solved
arranged	generated	motivated	streamlined
coordinated	implemented	organized	supervised
created	increased	planned	transformed
developed	initiated	prepared	utilized
doubled	launched	revised	verified
established	led	reduced	won

Working in pairs, use some of these power verbs in sentences to describe your past accomplishments to a fellow student. After you have made a general statement, give an example and quantify it. For example:

I implemented a new accounting system [*general statement*] that reduced the time necessary to prepare the balance sheet by 30 percent, thus saving the company $30,000 each year [*quantification*].

Even if you do not have a lot of experience, try to invent the kinds of accomplishments that will allow you to use power verbs.

WRITING: RÉSUMÉS AND COVER LETTERS

Write a cover letter and résumé to apply for the job your group selected. If you are currently a student, write the cover letter and résumé as if you had already completed your course of study. If you are already employed, write the cover letter and résumé to reflect your present status.

In addition to the advice given in Appendix 2 on Business Writing, consider the following tips.

Use quality paper (20–24 lb. bond).

Keep your résumé and cover letter short.

Always have someone proofread your résumé and cover letter.

Stress past accomplishments, promotions, and relevant skills.

Show, do not tell, and quantify results. For example, do not say "I am a hard worker." Instead state, "While maintaining a 3.25 average, I worked 20 hours a week as an on-campus sales representative for Graduation Rings, Inc., increasing sales by 25 percent over the previous representative.

Résumés

The layout of a résumé is extremely important. Use bold type for headings, and use proper spacing to make your résumé easy to read. Arrange the layout to place your strongest areas at the top. If you have a strong academic career but not much work experience, place "Education" at the top of the résumé. Remember to include activities that show your initiative and skills, even if you were not paid for these activities. For example, emphasize responsibilities associated with campus activities or civic groups. Write concisely and clearly. See the sample résumé shown in Figure 1-1.

Cover Letters

The cover letter should be addressed to a specific person, not just "Marketing Manager." The tone of your cover letter is extremely important. Once again, showing what you have done and quantifying your successes are excellent ways of presenting yourself positively without seeming overconfident. Present the relevant material, and let the receiver formulate a judgment. Do not tell him or her that you are the perfect candidate, but demonstrate your strengths through your accomplishments. An outline of a cover letter is provided below. You should review examples of cover letters that other people have prepared to help you develop your own.

FIRST PARAGRAPH: State why you are writing, what position you are applying for, where you heard about the position, and, briefly, why you would like to work for this company. For example, Joseph Daniels (whose résumé appears in Figure 1-1) might state that he heard a presentation of X company during a guest lecture in the series he arranged, was impressed by the company's success, and noted that they have several major accounts in Latin America.

SECOND PARAGRAPH: Discuss the relevance of your education, related activities, and projects to the job in question. Joseph Daniels might mention relevant marketing and Spanish courses, attempting to show how they help qualify him for the position. He could also mention his activities in the American Marketing Association.

THIRD PARAGRAPH: Discuss the relevance of your work experience. Joseph Daniels would emphasize his production, marketing, and sales experience and give any details that do not show up on his résumé.

FOURTH PARAGRAPH: Indicate your desire for a personal interview and your flexibility as to the time and place. A standard closing paragraph might be: I realize that a résumé cannot completely convey my background and qualifications. I would therefore welcome the opportunity to meet with you in person to present myself in more detail. I hope to hear from you soon and to be considered for the position of _____ .

VOCABULARY

You should be able to use these words, as well as the power verbs mentioned previously, in a job search situation.

to apply (in person/in writing), *v.*
applicant, *n.*
application, *n.*

appointment, *n.*
meeting, *n.*
conference, *n.*

B.A., *n.*
MBA, *n.*

boss, *n.*
supervisor, *n.*
immediate superior, *n.*

cover letter, *n.*

to employ, *v.*
employment, *n.*
employer, *n.*
employee, *n.*

fringe benefits, *n.* (expense account, health insurance, dental insurance, paid vacation, paid sick leave, parental leave, free telephone)

full-time, *adj.*
part-time, *adj.*

to graduate from, *v.*
a graduate of the University of California, *n.*

to hire, *v.*

interview, *n.*
to interview, *v.*

position, *n.*
previous/former, *adj.* (Example: *my former boss*)
present/current, *adj.*
future, *adj.*

profession, *n.*
occupation, *n.*
career, *n.* (career goals/long-range plans)

to promote, *v.*
promotion, *n.*
raise in salary, *n.*

required, *adj.*
preferred, *adj.*

résumé, *n.* (career objective, educational background, work experience, references, hobbies and activities, special qualifications)

salary (British: **wages**), n.

self-improvement, *n.*
to upgrade skills, *v.*

temporary, *adj.*
permanent, *adj.*

INVESTMENT

Portfolio Development

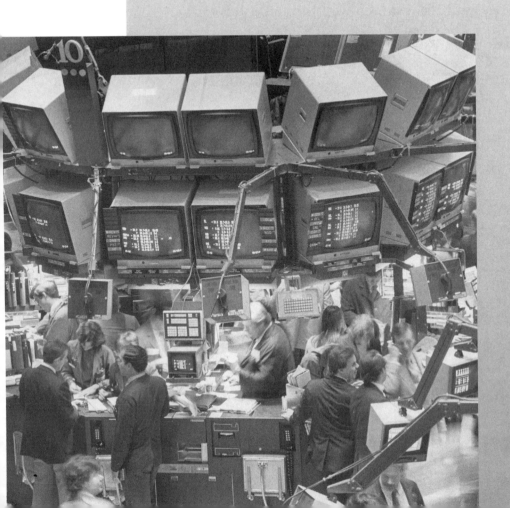

CULTURAL BACKGROUND: STOCKS, BONDS, AND MUTUAL FUNDS

Investment, particularly in individual stocks, bonds, and mutual funds, is common in both the United States and Britain, and about 20 percent of both populations own stocks. There is very little criticism of this way of making money in either of these countries, and, especially in the United States, with its emphasis on free enterprise, profit from investment is not criticized. Whereas making interest on loans is not accepted in certain cultures, it is perfectly acceptable in Anglo/American cultures. Even radical British unions have placed pension fund money in investments. But even within these cultures, there can be extremes, as we saw in the 1980s, when even very young businesspeople made fortunes as both brokers and investors; in many cases, these fortunes led to extravagant lifestyles, many of which ended abruptly with the market crash of 1987. Some Americans are gamblers and "Get rich quick" schemes have always been popular in the U.S. However, getting rich quickly can lead people to forget about the morality and legality of the things they did to get rich. It is interesting to note that two of the leading figures in the financial world during the 1980s went to jail for their practices. For those of you who come from cultures without a historical tradition of free enterprise, the idea of buying stocks may seem very foreign; however, it is definitely an accepted part of Western culture.

CASE

The purpose of this case is (a) to familiarize you with the English terminology for various investment instruments, and (b) to give you an opportunity to make a presentation in which you have to explain and defend your own investment choices. The presentation will give you the opportunity to use the basic vocabulary of the standard investment instruments: stocks, bonds, futures, puts and calls, mutual funds, and precious metals. Naturally, you will not be expected to learn all of the words in the vocabulary list. Rather, you should use it as a reference guide to provide you with the vocabulary you need to develop and present your portfolio. You may or may not be familiar with investment instruments. However, your presentations will increase your knowledge of some of these instruments, as well as give you insights into how they can be exploited profitably.

It would be wise to do this case early in the class, because that would provide more time to chart the result of the portfolios and run a contest to determine the best portfolio in the class. Naturally, the length of the class will affect your investment strategy. But you might also state in your presentation that your strategy is based on a longer term than just the length of the class, and then go on to explain your portfolio in light of this long-term investment strategy.

POINTS FOR DISCUSSION

1. Discuss investment strategies including:
   a) A breakdown of your portfolio in terms of the various instruments mentioned on pages 15 – 16. What percentage of your portfolio should be in stocks (and what types of stocks), precious metals, and so on? Why? [*For advanced students only.*]
   b) A strategy for a new investor with limited capital. [*For advanced students only.*]
2. What is the general attitude toward investment in your country? What are the most popular forms of investment, if any?
3. What sectors (such as oil and gas, biotechnology, auto industry, and so on) do you think will do well in the immediate future, and why?

CASE ACTIVITIES

Developing a Portfolio

You have $50,000 to invest (you can convert this to local currency if necessary). Meet with a fellow student who will act as a broker — preferably someone who has finance and investment as a specialty. Work out your investment goals and strategy and then develop a portfolio to meet these goals. You may use as many of the instruments (stocks, bonds, futures, puts and calls, and so on) as you feel will serve your goal. But remember the old adage, "Don't put all your eggs in one basket." Keeping this adage in mind, develop a portfolio. Your teacher will choose some of you to present your portfolios to the class and discuss why they are or are not sound. Thus, you will need to do some research.

Presentation

Those students chosen to present their portfolios will complete the following steps:

1. Explain your investment goals and strategies.
2. Present your portfolio and defend its soundness. For example, what types of investments were chosen, and what percentage of the $50,000 was allotted to each instrument (for example, 30 percent in stocks, 10 percent in precious metals, and so on)?

3. Explain your individual choices in detail. For example, provide the following information: (a) stocks (describe the growth potential, such as how much the price of the stock will rise); (b) dividends (how much interest, if any, will be paid on your investment); (c) the status of the company (as presented in its annual report); (d) the strength of the sector(s) (such as oil and biotechnology) that the company operates in, and so on. Provide information for mutual funds including the fund's past performance and the strength of the sectors emphasized in the fund, bonds, precious metals, and so on.

Your presentation should be complete with overheads or flipcharts to represent your information graphically. Remember, at the same time you are presenting your portfolio, you are also giving your fellow students valuable investment tips and techniques for investment analysis and portfolio development.

Students with a limited knowledge of securities markets, limit your portfolios to stocks. This will allow you to complete the exercise while not requiring a detailed knowledge of the securities markets.

Students with a more in-depth knowledge of securities markets, develop portfolios with several types investments. The following information should be given for each type of investment:

STOCKS

Price/earnings ratio and other annual report data relevant to the soundness of the company

Dividends

Charts based on past performance to identify price trends and cyclical movements

Special details about the company that might make it attractive, including (a) technological breakthroughs and new products, (b) a prospective takeover, (c) estimated profits, (d) book value per share that is significantly higher than the trading price of the shares, and (e) the past and expected performance of the sector (such as oil and gas, biotechnology, or airlines) of your stocks.

BONDS

Interest rates (fixed or not)

Whether or not the interest is taxed

Maturity date

Yield to maturity

The likelihood of the bond being called in

Par value versus present value

Bond interest rate versus its present price

FUTURES: [*For advanced students only.*]

Currency Futures

Explain how the instrument works and why you have chosen the currency you have.

Commodity Futures

Explain how the instrument works and why you have chosen the commodities you have.

PUTS AND CALLS: [*For advanced students only.*]

Index Puts and Calls

Explain the instrument and why you have chosen the investment you have.

Give the market prognosis for the period up until the expiration date of your puts or calls. Explain the advantages and disadvantages with this type of investment.

Individual Stock Puts and Calls

Give the same information asked for under Index Puts and Calls.

MUTUAL FUNDS

Explain the investment strategy of the mutual fund you have chosen in terms of the holdings of the mutual fund.

Discuss the advantages and disadvantages of mutual funds.

PRECIOUS METALS

Explain which instrument you have chosen (such as bullion, coins, certificates, or precious metals mutual funds) and justify this choice.

Predict the trend for this instrument over the period for this exercise and discuss factors that will influence this trend.

LANGUAGE MASTERY EXERCISE

Language Development: Stocks

Use the terms in the lists below to describe the fluctuations of the stock prices represented in Figures 2-1 and 2-2.

Adjective	Noun	Verb	Adverb
a rapid	increase	to increase	rapidly
a substantial	rise	to rise	substantially
a steady	growth	to grow	steadily
a great	improvement	to improve	greatly
a slight	decrease	to decrease	slightly
a gradual	deterioration	to deteriorate	gradually
a sudden	drop	to drop	suddenly

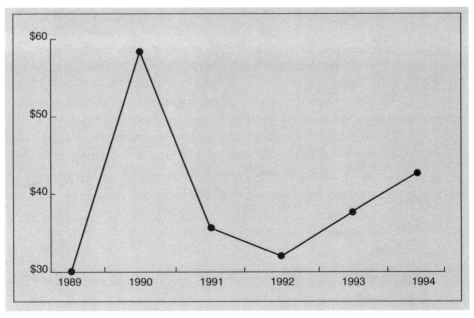

Figure 2-1   Transnational Financial Services Stock Price Fluctuation

a slow	decline	to decline	slowly
a dramatic	fall	to fall	dramatically
a noticeable	change	to change	noticeably

VOCABULARY

The following vocabulary list should give you the basic vocabulary to solve this case. However, you should also get a copy of an investment guide to improve your understanding of investment instruments. One such guide is *The Wall Street Journal: Guide to Understanding Money and Markets* (1990), available from Access Press Ltd., 10 East 53rd St., New York, NY 10022. The *Wall Street Journal* has also produced a videotape version of *Understanding Money and Markets*.

STOCKS (BRITISH: *SHARES*)

blue chips, *n.*   Stocks in large companies (such as AT&T) that are consistently profitable.

common stock, *n.*   Stock in a company that has second priority in terms of dividend distribution. **Preferred stock** holders receive dividends first and then the remainder of funds allotted to dividends (if any) is distributed to the common stockholders.

dividend, *n.*   A percentage of the profits of a company paid to stockholders. Stocks that consistently pay high dividends are known as **income stocks** and are generally considered a more conservative investment compared to **growth**

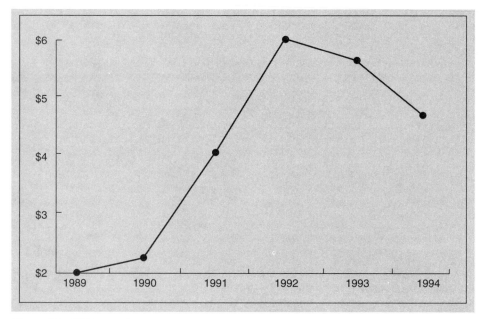

Figure 2-2   Wildcat Drilling Services Stock Price Fluctuations

stocks, which are bought in hopes that the price of the stock will rise. Growth companies often reinvest their profits and pay little or no dividends.

fundamental analysis, *n.*   An analysis of a stock based on the company's financial condition, products, and their sectors' growth potential.

par, *n.*   The face value of the shares at the time they were issued.

penny stocks, *n.*   Highly speculative, low-priced stocks for which the investment risk but also the profit potential is high.

price-earnings (P-E) ratio, *n.*   The ratio of the price of one share of stock to the annual earnings of the company per share. On the New York Stock Exchange, an average P-E ratio of about 18 : 1 or lower is considered positive.

technical analysis, *n.*   An analysis of a stock based on technical factors such as cyclical movement and price trends.

BONDS

asset-backed bonds, *n.*   Bonds backed by assets. Examples are **mortgage-backed bonds** and **equipment bonds**.

bearer bonds, *n.*   Bonds whose owner usually claims interest payments by sending in coupons.

bills, *n.*   Bonds that mature in one year or less.

bond rating, *n.* Rating services such as Moody's and Standard and Poor's rate bonds on a scale of AAA (highest quality) to C (lowest quality). (Remember that if the issuing organization goes bankrupt there is a strong likelihood that you will lose your money.) Bond ratings will also affect yield, as bonds with high ratings usually pay lower interest rates.

bond yield, *n.*   Not the same as the interest rate. At par value (say $1000) the interest rate and yield will be the same, let us say 8 percent. However, if the value drops to $800, the yield will rise, as the holder will still receive $80 (8 percent of the par value of $1000), even though the bond only costs $800 — producing a yield of 10 percent.

callable bonds, *n.*   Bonds that can be **redeemed** (*v.*, paid off) prior to the due date.

convertible bonds, *n.*   Bonds that pay interest but also give the right to convert the bonds to the company's stocks as a means of repayment of the loan. The terms of conversion are stated in the bond agreement. Of particular importance is the conversion price — how much will have to be paid for each share of stock when converting the bond to stock.

coupons, *n.*   Attached numbered or dated sections of the bond, which provide a method of redeeming the interest due at various intervals.

debenture bond, *n.*   A bond that is backed only by the credit of the organization issuing it and not by any assets guaranteeing its repayment.

discount, *n.*   A bond that is selling for less than its par value.

interest rate, *n.*   The percentage of the par value that will be paid to the bondholder on a regular basis.

junk bonds, *n.*   A low-grade bond with high interest, a highly popular invention of the 1980s. Many of these junk bonds are now in default.

maturity date, *n.*   When the loan will be paid off (that is, the bondholder will get his or her money back).

par value, *n.*   The amount the bondholder will be paid at the bond's maturity.

premium, *n.*   A bond that is selling for more than its par value.

registered bonds, *n.*   Bonds registered in someone's name; interest payments to the owner occur automatically.

t-bills (British: guilts), *n.*   Bonds issued by the United States Treasury or the Bank of England.

zero-coupon bonds, *n.*   Bonds that pay no interest while the loan is outstanding; however, the interest does **accrue** (*v.*, to build up) and is paid out at maturity. To encourage investors to buy these bonds they are offered at **deep discounts** (prices much lower than their par value.)

MUTUAL FUNDS

diversification, *n.*   One reason to buy mutual funds. A mutual fund is a portfolio that is managed by professionals and spreads the investment across a wide number of stocks, allowing for **diversified investment**. A person who buys into a mutual fund buys a small part of an already diversified portfolio and receives professional management services at the same time.

load funds, *n.*   Funds that charge a commission (up to 8.5 percent) when you invest and withdraw money.

no-load funds, *n.*   Funds that do not charge sales commissions. However, *all* funds charge a management fee of from 0.5 percent to 1 percent, and some charge a withdrawal fee.

FUNDS AND THEIR OBJECTIVES

aggressive growth funds, *n.*   Funds that invest in newer companies or companies with new management that the fund's managers feel can turn these companies around. The potential price rise is high, but safety is low to very low. The goal is maximum price rise.

balanced funds, *n.*   Funds that invest in a combination of bonds, and preferred and common stock. The goal is current income and long-term growth (price rise) and safety.

fixed income and equity income funds, *n.*   Funds that invest in stocks and bonds that provide high interest and dividends. The goal is high current income, but the disadvantage is low capital gains potential.

growth and income funds, *n.*   Funds that invest in companies with a solid track record and a record of dividend payment. Yield is both from **capital gains** (price rise) and dividends. Both the safety and potential income are moderate. Your goal is a combination of price rise and dividend income.

growth funds, *n.*   Funds that invest in common stock of settled companies. The potential price rise is high, but the safety is low. The goal is high **capital gains** (profit made by the increased price of your stock).

money market and government money market funds, *n.*   Funds that invest in short-term debt securities. The goal is current income and maximum safety. The disadvantage is no potential price rise.

FUTURES

commodities, *n.*   Raw materials that go into the production of products. Examples are oil, pork bellies, grains, and precious metals (such as gold, silver, and platinum).

futures contracts, *n.*   Contracts made now for a transaction in the future. The main details of the future are the commodity to be bought, the future price, and the future date by which the transaction has to be exercised.

to go long, *v.*   To take a buyer's position.

to go short, *v.*   To take a seller's position.

hedgers and **speculators,** *n.*   The two major players in the futures market. *Hedgers*, such as farmers, for example, are just trying to insure getting a fixed price for their goods to insure a predetermined profit margin at a future date. Other hedgers could be manufacturers who will need commodities for future production and want to factor in costs now as part of their cost accounting. *Speculators* try to make a profit by guessing where various commodity markets are going.

leverage, *n.* Using a little money to control a much larger investment. For example, if you were going to buy 42,000 gallons of oil you would have to pay around $20,000 at today's price. But buying a future will give you the right to buy this amount at a future date. Let us say that the future to buy 42,000 gallons of oil at $22 a barrel costs $100. Let us also say that oil shot up to $25 a barrel and your future was worth $3 (actually, it would probably be worth more if people expected the price of oil to continue to go up). A barrel of oil is 42 gallons, so your one contract (see definition below) means you can buy 1,000 barrels of oil at $22 a barrel and sell it immediately for $25 a barrel, thus realizing a profit of $3,000 on a $100 investment. This is much more than if you had bought and stored the 42,000 gallons of oil. The disadvantage of futures is that if the price goes the other way, you can be forced to buy commodities at a higher price than the current market price.

one contract, *n.* Represents the right to buy or sell a specific quantity of a commodity. For example, one contract of oil = 42,000 gallons; one contract of wheat = 5,000 bushels.

OPTIONS

calls, *n.* The right to buy a certain commodity, stock, or currency at an agreed price, called the strike price, up until an agreed time, called the expiration date.

index options, *n.* You can buy puts and calls on the index, which means that you are betting that the index will go up (*calls*) or down (*puts*). The standard index options in the United States are on the Standard and Poor's Index. Think how much money you would have made in October 1987 during the market crash if you had bought puts!

options, *n.* Like futures, options offer the right to buy or sell something at a designated date, but you do not have to exercise this option. If, for example, you have an option to buy a security at $20 and it is selling at $18 at the expiration date, there is no point in exercising your option. Thus, you don't, and you simply lose the money you have paid for the option.

option premium, *n.* A form of commission that the buyer pays the seller for this kind of transaction. However, the seller is committed to meet the terms of the transaction if the buyer chooses to exercise his or her option. If the option gives the right to buy a security at a certain price, the seller must obtain that security at the market price and sell it to the holder of the option at the price agreed upon in the option. For example, if the holder of an option to buy a security at $18 exercises the option when the security is at $20, he or she gains $2 per option at the expense of the seller, who must obtain the security at $20 and sell it at $18 to the holder of the option.

puts, *n.* The right to sell according to the same conditions described for calls.

FINANCE

Other People's Money:
Larry the Liquidator vs.
New England Wire
and Cable

CULTURAL BACKGROUND: FREE ENTERPRISE

The American play *Other People's Money* illustrates the extremes of a free enterprise system in which corporate raiders take over a company against the company's will and *strip* it (sell off or close down divisions of the company for quick profit). The play raises questions about how "free" a free enterprise system that lets a few rich people profit at the expense of the many who lose their jobs really is. It also raises questions about the need for more restrictions on the activities of corporate raiders. What has happened to the distinction between making an honest profit from investment and making a fortune by stripping a company?

CASE

This case is based on Jerry Sterner's play *Other People's Money*, which has now been made into a movie of the same name. A prerequisite for solving this case is to have read the play or seen the movie. If you chose the latter, remember that Hollywood has naturally chosen a happy ending, whereas, in the play, the factory in question is shut down and all the workers lose their jobs—a more realistic conclusion to this scenario. As you will discover, Larry "the Liquidator" Garfinkle is a Wall Street raider who thrives on takeovers, usually hostile ones. He spots companies, such as New England Wire and Cable, whose book value per share far exceeds their stock price. He starts buying up the shares in a move to take over the company. His buy-up pleases the stockholders, who see him as the reason for the increased value of their stock and often support him in the takeover.

The negative aspect of Larry the Liquidator's activities is that his only real concern is the book value of the company; thus, once the takeover is completed, he is likely to strip the company, closing down unprofitable or marginally profitable operations and selling off other operations. As his nickname indicates, he liquidates companies to realize their book value, an operation which can result in quick profits. Another result, however, is unemployment and the ripple effect that it creates in the communities where factories are closed. The leveraged buyouts necessary to take over some companies can produce another negative effect as well. The resulting debt level makes streamlining of operations and modernizing the equipment impossible, because there is no capital available for this due to the high debt levels. Ironically, the streamlining of operations is often given as the reason for the takeover, but such streamlining is made impossible by the debt levels incurred in the takeover.

POINTS FOR DISCUSSION

After having seen or read the movie or play, you should be ready to discuss the following topics:

1. Do you feel, as does Jorgensen, that the board of directors has a social responsibility to the workers and the local community? Or do you side with Garfinkle, maintaining that the directors' only responsibility is to the stockholders and thus to maximize profits? If you side with Jorgensen, how far are you willing to go in subsidizing jobs at a factory that is losing money?

2. After his buy-up is temporarily stopped by a court injunction, Garfinkle complains about the present state of capitalism. He rants on about lawyers and others who are destroying the capitalist system. He feels that anyone should have the right to buy out any company he wishes. He feels that the fact that he is not allowed to buy up and do whatever he wants with a company (including selling off part of it for a quick profit and even closing down factories, thus throwing people into unemployment) shows that the capitalist system is being destroyed.

   a) First, discuss Garfinkle's concept of a free market and whether or not you agree with it.

   b) Second, discuss whether it is government regulations, such as the injunction imposed on Garfinkle, or raiders like Garfinkle who pose the greatest threat to the capitalist system. Be specific about what restrictions, if any, you feel should be placed on raiders like Garfinkle.

3. Would Garfinkle's activities be allowed in your country?

CASE ACTIVITIES

Roleplay: New England Wire and Cable's Annual Meeting

Dramatize the annual meeting of New England Wire and Cable. Annual meetings give the stockholders the opportunity to voice their opinions on issues of importance to the company. In this meeting, the stockholders have to decide whether they support the current management headed by Jorgensen or the team headed by Garfinkle. One team of students will assume the roles of the present management, including Jorgensen, Coles, a representative from the workers, and a local politician. All of them will speak in favor of retaining the present board of directors. The second team will take on the roles of Garfinkle and his lawyers. After both sides have presented their cases, the stockholders, who will be played by the remaining members of the class, can ask questions of the two teams. Finally, the stockholders will vote for one of the two teams to assume the management of New England Wire and Cable. They can either be assigned the same amount of

REPORT FOR THE STOCKHOLDERS MEETING*
February 27, 199__

Market Prognosis

As loyal stockholders, many of you know that New England Wire and Cable has performed only moderately well for the past decade. However, we have survived these difficult times and have great plans and prospects for the future. We have survived numerous recessions, a major depression and two World Wars. To allow a company with such a history of survival to be taken over and broken up for its value by a man who cares for nothing but money would be devastating to this community and detrimental to the industrial infrastructure of our nation. Our industrial strength and manufacturing capabilities continue to be stolen and disbanded by these mergers and acquisitions specialists interested only in making money. They make nothing and contribute even less to our economy. At least the robber barons of old left something in their wake. These men leave nothing but a blizzard of paper to cover the pain.

Can you, in good conscience, allow this man to destroy this company just because its value dead is greater than its value alive at this point in time? While this may be true for now, are you willing to sacrifice the possibility of even greater future benefits for a single payment? The new $150 billion transportation bill has designated federal funds to be spent on rebuilding our nation's highways and bridges. This means a potential for New England Wire and Cable to operate with considerable profits. As you know, the parent company, New England Wire and Cable, has been operating with a loss recently, including a $3 million loss last year, while the remaining companies have been operating with significant profits, which allowed us to report a net income of $125,000. However, the construction activity that the transportation bill will generate will result, according to our prognosis, in a profit of $1 million already this year. The estimated profits for New England Wire and Cable based on the activity generated by the transportation bill <u>alone</u> will be $10 million over the next five years.

This possible takeover has also sparked us, as the management team, to examine our operations and determine what we can do to improve the op-

continued

---

*A report to the stockholders is an evaluation by management of the past year's performance of the company and a prediction of its future success.

continued

erations and profitability of our company. We have concluded that it will be entirely feasible for us to restructure and consolidate in such a manner that we will be able to save significant amounts of money through a reduction in operating expenses.

While the offer presented to all of you stockholders may be very attractive, I hope that you will be able to look beyond the immediate capital gains and vote for the future of New England Wire and Cable, our local community, and American industry.

ANDREW JORGENSEN
Chairman

shares or varying amounts of shares. After the vote is taken, students selected randomly will be asked to justify why they voted as they did.

The accompanying report states management's analysis of the company's present financial situation based on the balance sheet shown in Figure 3-1 and a forecast of future prospects. Naturally, it favors the present management's position.

Garfinkle's argument appeals to the stockholders on the basis of quick profit in that he will offer more money for each share than its current value on the stock exchange.

LANGUAGE MASTERY EXERCISE

Meeting Terminology and Procedures

The following statements include standard meeting terminology, which Jorgensen would use in *chairing* (leading) the meeting. Learn them in preparation for your dramatization of the meeting.

OPENING THE MEETING

I declare the meeting open.

APPROVAL OF THE ANNUAL REPORT

Are there any additions, corrections, or questions concerning the annual report and the accounts?

THE AGENDA

The main item on the agenda is the question of the election of a new board of directors.

NEW ENGLAND WIRE AND CABLE
Balance Sheet
December 31, 19——

Assets

Current Assets

Cash	$10,000,000
Accounts Receivable	6,000,000
Inventories	12,000,000
U.S. Govt. and other marketable securities	2,000,000

Total Current Assets $30,000,000

Property, Plant, and Equipment

Land	$100,000
Equipment	120,000,000
Building	500,000
Accumulated Depreciation: Equipment	60,000,000
Accumulated Depreciation: Building	400,000

Total PP and E $60,200,000

Total Assets $90,200,000

Liabilities and Stockholders' Equity

Current Liabilities

Accounts Payable	$2,200,000
Accrued Taxes (other than income taxes)	250,000
Accrued Compensation and Benefits	50,000
Advances from Customers on Contract	2,500,000

Total Current Liabilities   5,000,000

continued

Figure 3-1 Balance sheet

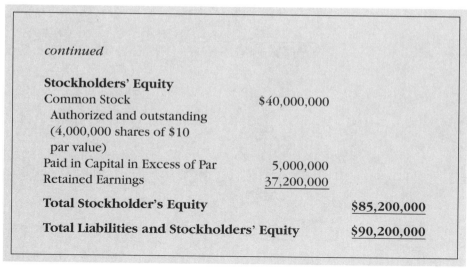

Stockholders' Equity
Common Stock	$40,000,000
Authorized and outstanding	
(4,000,000 shares of $10	
par value)	
Paid in Capital in Excess of Par	5,000,000
Retained Earnings	37,200,000

Total Stockholder's Equity	**$85,200,000**
Total Liabilities and Stockholders' Equity	**$90,200,000**

Figure 3-1   Balance sheet *(continued)*

NEW ENGLAND WIRE AND CABLE
Combined Statement of Income
and Retained Earnings
For the Year Ended December 31, 19 ____

Sales Revenue	$20,000,000
Cost of Goods Sold	13,750,000
Depreciation Expense	2,000,000
Compliance Expense	2,500,000
Selling and Administrative Expenses	1,625,000
Net Income	**$125,000**
Retained Earnings Jan. 1	37,200,000
Cash Dividends Declared and Paid	125,000
Retained Earnings Dec. 31	$37,200,000

Combined Statement of Income and Retained Earnings

OPENING THE FLOOR TO DEBATE

After both teams have made their presentations, an announcement such as the following is made.

The floor is hereby open to debate.

GIVING THE FLOOR

Having the floor means having the right to speak.

> Mr. X now has the floor.

POINT OF ORDER

When someone questions whether proper meeting procedure is being followed, he or she is raising a point of order.

> Point of order, Mr. Chairman; I believe I was next on the list of speakers, not Ms. Y.

POINT OF INFORMATION

Inserting a point of information allows someone the right to ask a question relevant to the present discussion without putting his or her name on the speakers' list and waiting for his or her turn.

> Point of information. I would like to know what Mr. Garfinkle intends to do with this factory here in Pawtucket if he takes over the company.

KEEPING ORDER

If someone does not adhere to the proper rules of procedure for a meeting, the chairperson can rule that person is out of order.

> Order, order. Mr. W, you are out of order. It is not your turn to speak.

MAKING A PROPOSAL OR A MOTION

> I propose that we. . . .
> I move that we. . . .

SECONDING A PROPOSAL

Once a formal proposal or motion has been made, it must have a *second* — that is, one other person who supports the proposal or motion.

> I second the motion.

CALLING FOR THE VOTE

When the chairperson or any other participant in the meeting with voting rights feels that an item has been discussed sufficiently, he or she can call for the vote. If there are no objections, then the chairperson can move on to the vote. If there are objections, a vote must be taken to conclude discussion. If over 50 percent of those present with voting rights vote for concluding the discussion, then they can go on to the final vote. If not, the discussion of the item in question continues.

PARTICIPANT: I call for the vote.

CHAIRPERSON: Are there any objections? [No objections are raised.] Hearing no objections, we will now proceed to the vote.

SECRET BALLOT

The vote will be determined by secret ballot, so please fill out your ballots and hand them in to Mr. Coles.

THE RESULT OF THE VOTE

The ballots have been counted and the results are: Mr. Jorgensen and the present board of directors,   votes; Mr. Garfinkle   votes.

ADJOURNING THE MEETING

After all business is completed, the meeting is *adjourned* (called to a close).

The meeting is adjourned.

All students should be familiar with the above terms. The person who plays Jorgensen will actively use all of them during the meeting.

WRITING: RESPONSES TO THE ANNUAL MEETING

One group must take notes from the meeting and write a report summarizing the two presentations and the result of the vote to be sent to the stockholders. Another group can write a newspaper article about the meeting. The article should give a brief summary of the two side's positions, questions that were raised by stockholders, the result of the vote, and what the decision will mean for the local community. The teacher will assign these two writing projects to two groups prior to the meeting.

The competing factions should write up the presentations they gave at the annual meeting, and the remaining students should write a justification of why they voted as they did.

VOCABULARY

acquisition, *n.*   The act of acquiring a business.

assets, *n.*   All things owned by a person or business that have some monetary value.

book value, *n.*   The value of an asset or group of assets of a business as shown in its account books.

buy-out, *n.*   The buying of the entire interest in a business.

buy-up, *n.*   The buying of as many of the shares of a company as one can buy, usually to get control of the company.

capital, *n.*   Accumulated wealth or property used in the production of further wealth.

cash cow, *n.*   A company which can be "milked" (take out as much money as possible).

cash flow, *n.*   Cash generated and used in operations.

Chapter 11 (American), *n.* A provision in the federal bankruptcy law which allows a financially troubled company to postpone payment to creditors while it works out a plan to repay them.

court injunction, *n.* A court order prohibiting an action (in this case preventing Garfinkle from buying more New England Wire and Cable shares).

debt, *n.* The amount, usually of money, owed by one person or business to others, known as **creditors**.

healthy company, *n.* A financially sound company.

hostile takeover, *n.* Any takeover unwanted by the present management.

in play, *adj.* Used to describe a company which is a target of a takeover.

junk bonds, *n.* Low-grade bonds with high interest often used for leveraged buy-outs.

lean and mean, *adj.* Used to describe a company or organization that reduces its work force by getting rid of "deadwood" (unproductive employees) in order to be more profitable.

leveraged buy-outs (LBO), *n.* Buying a company with borrowed funds, using the company itself as collateral.

to liquidate, *v.* To sell off a company's assets.

M and A, *n.* Mergers and acquisitions.

merger, *n.* The combining of two or more companies.

raiders, *n.* People who look for companies that they can buy cheaply, often with the thought of stripping them.

ripple effect, *n.* The spreading effects caused by an event.

shark repellent, *n.* Something that makes a company in play less attractive to a raider. For example, if the board of directors substantially increased the dividend, it would encourage the stockholders to hold onto their stocks while reducing the capital in the company, thus making a raid not only more difficult but less attractive.

to strip, *v.* To buy up cheaply companies that are showing poor results, then sell off the assets one by one at a profit and close down the business.

to take private, *v.* A move by management to buy up the stock of its company so that it is not traded on the stock exchange. This is done to prevent a hostile takeover and is usually financed through a leveraged buy-out.

takeover, *n.* The act of gaining control of a company by making its shareholders a general offer, through an action called a **takeover bid**.

tender offer takeover, *n.* A hostile takeover not negotiated with the management of the target firm. The offer is usually made directly to the stockholders of the targeted firm.

white knight, *n.* A friendly acquirer who is sought by the target of a hostile takeover bid.

working capital, *n.* The excess of total current assets over total current liabilities. It represents the net amount of a company's relatively liquid resources and the margin of safety available to meet the financial demands of the operating cycle.

REFERENCES

The following articles provide important information for the class discussion and the solution of this case. You should read them or similar articles.

Barlett, Donald L. and James B. Steele. "Simplicity Pattern: Irresistible to Raiders," In *America: What Went Wrong?* Andrews and McMeel. Kansas City: 1992.

Faltermayer, Edmund. "The Deal Decade: Verdict on the '80s." *Fortune* (August 26, 1991): 58–70.

MARKETING
NEGOTIATIONS

Long-range Golf Equipment Seeks a Distributor

CULTURAL BACKGROUND: CUSTOMS IN AMERICAN NEGOTIATION

Each culture has different ways of approaching negotiations. Being a negotiator in international negotiations requires an understanding of the way other nations' negotiating teams think and function. Books have been written on the subject of national differences in negotiating, but it is important to remember that even within a given culture, each negotiating team will vary from national norms. In negotiating, one must be aware of national traits and customs, while looking for individual variation. However, certain traits do appear, and the following list describes typical American traits.

TIME: Negotiations should begin on time. "Time is money" and thus negotiations should not take more time than necessary. This means that American negotiators are sometimes frustrated by what they may perceive as "Latin time," in which meetings tend not to start at the scheduled time. They may also be frustrated by the Arab tendency to want to establish friendship before negotiations can really begin or to allow negotiations to be interrupted by other business. Americans are very goal-oriented, set up time schedules, and hope to conclude negotiations within those time schedules; as a result, they can appear to be impatient or "pushy" (to pressure the opposite side to come to an agreement).

CONTRACT: Americans look at negotiations as a means of reaching a contract; thus they tend to stress legality and the binding nature of a written document setting out rights and duties that can be upheld in a court of law. Other cultures look at negotiations as a means of establishing a relationship which will be the basis of future business arrangements. For Americans, a contract is the sign of closing a deal, while for some cultures it begins a relationship. The American emphasis on a binding legal document may be interpreted by other cultures as a lack of trust.

PROTOCOL: *Protocol* refers to the formal aspects of negotiations. It includes such matters as how to address people (by first or last names), the use of titles, dress, gift giving, exchange of business cards, respect for age, the shape of the negotiating table and the placement of negotiators, and so on. Americans are informal and might overlook the importance of protocol, which can be interpreted as impoliteness.

DECISION MAKING: The decision-making process might be individual, authoritarian, or by consensus. While in American teams, the decision-making power often lies in the hands of individuals, other cultures emphasize group agreement, or *consensus*, which naturally takes longer.

DIRECT OR INDIRECT COMMUNICATION: Americans value directness and tend to say right out what they mean. For other cultures, especially those concerned with saving face, such directness can be embarrassing. Americans tend to ask direct questions and expect direct answers, whereas other cultures often respond through signs, gestures, and what may appear to Americans as vague comments.

CONFLICT: Conflict is not seen as necessarily negative for American negotiators; rather, it is often seen as an expected part of the negotiating process. Negative emotions are perhaps more acceptable to Americans than in some Asian cultures. Thus, American negotiators can appear more confrontational than their Asian counterparts.

WIN-WIN VERSUS WIN-LOSE: Win-win refers to a win for both sides, while win-lose describes a situation in which one side benefits at the other side's expense. The emphasis in the United States on winning may tend to push American negotiators toward win-lose strategies. Another factor is the U. S. tendency to emphasize the individual rather than the group, which can lead American negotiators to value individual interests more highly than collective interests.

BODY LANGUAGE: Americans look each other directly in the eyes, which may be considered impolite in other countries. On the other hand, if someone does *not* look an American negotiator directly in the eyes, the American may consider this a reason for distrust. Signs and gestures may have less importance in American negotiations than in negotiations from cultures where indirect communication is important.

CASE

Distributing your products is one of the major aspects of marketing. Although it is possible to open up a sales office in foreign countries, most companies cannot afford the expense and choose instead to work with a foreign marketing agent. Dealing with an agent means that you can take advantage of his or her knowledge of consumer habits, advertising approaches, and existing distribution channels. However, this also involves negotiating contracts, which is the subject of this case.

Negotiating a contract for an ongoing business relationship is a delicate matter. Unlike selling a used car to someone whom you probably will never see again, an agency agreement must be mutually satisfying if you expect your agent to make a 100 percent effort to sell and distribute your products. Thus, pressuring the agent to give up $\frac{1}{4}$ percent on his or her commission might be like winning the battle, but losing the war. You win the $\frac{1}{4}$ percent, but weaken the business relationship. Naturally, you want to achieve the best possible result for your company, but at the same time you do not want to poison the ongoing business relationship on which your future success depends. Negotiations are a case of give-and-take, and good negotiators are sensitive to the priorities and requirements of the other side. Beating the other side into submission, even though it may give you a sense of victory, is certainly not the way to establish the atmosphere of mutual understanding necessary for an ongoing business relationship.

With this in mind, any contract preparation must take into consideration both parties in the agreement. Included in this case is a negotiation worksheet that you should fill out in advance of the actual negotiations you will conduct. What follows is a brief summary of how to go about filling out the negotiations worksheet.

I. Goals

In this particular case, you are going to be negotiating rates of commission, an exclusive versus a nonexclusive contract, a fixed price contract versus a flexible price contract, and the covering of advertising, shipping, and storage costs.

You must determine which of these items are high priority, which are medium priority, and which are low priority. For items in the latter two categories, you must determine how far you are willing to go in making concessions and what you expect to get in return for your concessions. Some of your low-priority points may be used as trading cards to be given away in their entirety in return for concessions from the other side. However, you should have a clear notion of what you expect to get in return.

II. An Assessment of the Balance of Power

Despite what was stated about the necessity of a mutually satisfying agreement, each side will evaluate the strengths and weaknesses of the other party involved in the negotiations in order to avoid being "steamrollered" (dominated by the other side). Assessment of the balance of power will help you in determining your strategy, including how much pressure you want to put on the other party (while not forgetting the importance of a mutually satisfying agreement). Some basic questions you have to ask are (a) How much do we need them, and (b) What alternatives do we have, and how viable are those alternatives? Naturally, you must also ask how much the other side needs *you*.

III. Determining Your Strategy

Your strategy should be a result of your decisions on points I and II. You must determine where the *bottom line* is; that is, how far you are willing to go to obtain an agreement, and what do you ideally hope to achieve? The final contract will fall somewhere between these two extremes, and charting them will give you a tool to evaluate the result. Maybe you will achieve a result closer to your ideal contract. There is nothing wrong with shooting for an ideal result, as long as your goals do not appear unreasonable, and as long as when you do meet resistance, you do not maintain an inflexible position. Ultimatums rarely get you anywhere.

Determine your opening position and the mood you hope to create. As mentioned in the worksheet, there are degrees of positions from hard-line to softer stances. Remember, however, this opening position will determine the atmosphere for the rest of the negotiations. So choose it with care.

Determine what issues you want to negotiate first. This will help set the tone. If you take the low-priority issues first, you will create a tone of flexibility and good faith. You may be able to create a tone of flexibility on both sides, making it easier for you to get what you want on the high-priority items later. Your strategy here would be to suggest that you have shown good faith and that now it is the other side's turn.

On the other hand, starting with your high-priority items will let you know early in the negotiations what the other side's stance is on those items most important to you. Remember, the sensitive negotiator will constantly be listening for clues as to the other side's position and priorities. Starting with your high-priority items may give you necessary clues as to the other party's position. If you do not meet resistance, go for the maximum, and once you have attained what you want, you can be flexible on some of the other items to "sweeten the pot," thus creating an atmosphere of mutual satisfaction. Remember, while you are negotiating, you are constantly listening for clues as to the other side's priorities, as well as how they perceive the balance of power. Thus, in the beginning, you might "go fishing" just to see what "bait" interests the other side. Once you see what interests them, you may be able to formulate a clear picture of their strategy.

This has hardly been an exhaustive study of negotiation strategy, and you should study the subject in more detail and discuss your experiences and strategies. However, this should give you enough information to solve this case. So fill out the negotiations worksheet, determine your strategy, and be sensitive to possible clues during the negotiations.

POINTS FOR DISCUSSION

1. Discuss any differences in approaches to negotiations within your culture in contrast to those described above. What problems could such differences create in negotiations with American negotiators?

2. Groups should be assigned a role as either long-range or XYZ. Then each group should discuss strategies for the case individually, including the following:
   a) What tone would you set for the negotiations (hard-line or flexible) and how would you do it?
   b) What are the most important items to be negotiated (commissions, an exclusive versus a nonexclusive contract, and so on)?
   c) Would you start the negotiations with your "musts" (high-priority items) or your "trading cards" (low-priority items); why?
   d) What is your attitude toward the opposing side, and how will that affect your negotiations strategy?

CASE ACTIVITIES

Negotiating a Distribution Contract

Long-range Sporting Goods, Inc., of Elizabeth, New Jersey, has contacted XYZ Distributors as a possible agent for their golf clubs and bags in your country (if the case is solved in the United States, choose a country for XYZ). Long-range produces a mid-to-luxury range of clubs and bags. Their emphasis, however, is on the up-market segment, and they emphasize quality. Thus, they are very interested in penetrating your country's market. Although a relative newcomer to the market, Long-range has enjoyed rapid success in the United States. By sponsoring some young and successful golf pros on the U.S. tour, they brought their sales from a modest $10 million in 1991 to an annual sales of $90 million last year. They feel that they have established their reputation in the U.S. market well enough to allow them to attempt a foreign market penetration. However, since their U.S. market is expanding and their profits are good, they do not wish to risk an expansion at any price.

XYZ Distributors is a medium-size distributor of U.S. sports equipment. They do not distribute any major brands of golf equipment, such as Wilson or Spalding. However, they have signed a three-year contract with Sigma and Hurricane which expires at the end of this year. They have enjoyed much success with Sigma and Hurricane, but they are looking for an opportunity to get in on the ground floor with Long-range. They have connections with pro shops and up-market golf shops, but have avoided shops at the lower end of the market.

For this case, half the groups will represent Long-range and the other half XYZ Distributors. You can have as many negotiations going on at once as you have teams and space.

The basic items in the contract to be decided are the following:

1. *An exclusive contract versus a nonexclusive contract.* In an exclusive contract, Long-range would demand that XYZ distribute only their line of golf equipment, thus dropping Tiger Shark and Hurricane. However, if XYZ accepts this demand, they could in turn demand exclusive rights to be the sole distributor of Long-range clubs and bags in this market.

2. *A fixed price contract versus a flexible price contract.* In a fixed price contract, the price of the goods is fixed once a year. In a flexible price contract, Long-range reserves the right to raise the price of clubs in accordance with a rise in production costs. Naturally, the distributor could, and probably would, have to pass the rise on to the golf shops. This could lead to friction between the distributor and the golf shops.

3. *The rate of commission to be paid the distributor based on FOB (free on board) New York.* You can negotiate a flat commission, such as 7 percent on all sales, or a sliding scale, such as 7 percent on sales up to $10 million and 8 percent on sales from $10 million to $20 million, and so on.

4. *The covering of advertising costs and procedures for approving advertising campaigns.* Who should cover these costs, and who will have the final decision about advertising campaigns?

5. *The covering of shipping expenses FOB New York and storage costs in your country.* Who should cover these costs?

You should negotiate a contract that establishes the conditions for these five points.

Presentation

Each group should be prepared to make a presentation describing (a) the contract arrived at, (b) their negotiating team's strategies and goals, and (c) how successful they were in attaining their goals in the final contract.

LANGUAGE MASTERY EXERCISE

Use the following Negotiations Worksheet and Report Format outline to organize, and report on, your negotiations process.

Negotiations Worksheet

I. YOUR GOALS: (A listing of the priority of the different areas to be negotiated.)

A. Decide on your high-priority items, and whether or not there is any room for negotiation concerning them.
B. Set bottom lines for those items that are negotiable.
C. Decide on "trading cards," (low-priority items) if any, and what you expect to get in return for giving up these items.
D. Decide in general what you expect to get in return for any concessions you make.
E. Set a bottom line for the contract as a whole.

II. AN ASSESSMENT OF THE BALANCE OF POWER

A. Evaluate what the other side stands to gain by this association, and what you stand to gain. Be sure to make a fair evaluation, in order to avoid a false sense of power.
  1. Evaluate what you can offer them in this deal, what they can offer you, and who needs whom the most.
B. Decide what you can say or do in the negotiations to impress on the other side your position of power (remembering all the time that you are walking a fine line between trying to attain your goals as completely as possible while still reaching a mutually satisfying agreement).

III. DETERMINATION OF STRATEGY BASED ON I AND II

A. Determine your opening stance, and make a summary of your opening statement.
  1. Is your position going to be flexible or hard-line?
  2. Do you have the power to enforce your position?

B. Decide whether to negotiate the high-priority items or the medium- and low-priority items first.

C. Decide whether to set any preconditions (always be careful on this point).

Report Format

See the section on the format of reports in Appendix 2 on Business Writing (pp. 135–137). Organize your negotiations progress report within the following sections:

1. Pre-Negotiations Strategy
   a) Goals
   b) Assessment of the balance of power
   c) The tone to be established at the beginning of the negotiations
   d) The order of discussion of the items (commissions, exclusive contract, and so on)
2. The Negotiations
   a) What occurred during the negotiations?
   b) Did the negotiations follow your strategy and how successful was your strategy?
3. The Tentative Contract Agreement Reached between XYZ and Long-range
   a) Commission
   b) Exclusive contract
   c) Fixed price versus flexible price contract
   d) Coverage of advertising costs and authority over advertising campaigns
   e) Coverage of shipping expenses
4. Recommendation
   a) Should your management accept the contract?
   b) What impact will this contract have on your company's earnings in the coming years?

WRITING: REPORT ON NEGOTIATION PROGRESS

In order to prepare a report on your group's progress in negotiations, first fill in your negotiations worksheet. Then, based on notes taken during the negotiation meeting, write a report to your respective board of directors using the guidelines above.

VOCABULARY

achieve, *v.*   To reach your goals. (Example: "We hope to achieve our goals of. . . .")

agreement, *n.*   Reaching a mutually acceptable compromise to which both sides agree.

balance of power, *n.*   An analysis of the strengths and weaknesses of both sides to determine which side has the strongest bargaining position.

bargaining, *n.* (**to bargain,** *v.*)   Negotiating with the purpose of coming to an agreement.

bargaining power, *n.*   The power of one's position in the process of negotiating.

bottom line, *n.*   The lowest you are willing to go to reach an agreement. (Also: the line at the bottom of a financial report showing profit or loss.)

concessions, *n.*   Compromises made by one side in order to reach an agreement. Concessions from one side are expected to be matched by concessions from the other side.

conditions, *n.*   The terms of a contract or the demands of the bargaining teams.

confirm, *v.*   To make certain. (Example: "We confirmed the date of the meeting.")

convince/persuade, *v.*   To get the other side to agree that your point of view is correct.

deadlocked, *adj.*   When the negotiating process cannot proceed because both sides are unwilling to compromise.

demands, *n.*   Your opening position in a negotiation; what you hope to achieve.

final offer, *n.*   Your last offer before breaking off negotiations.

flexible, *adj.*   Willing to negotiate, not rigid in your demands.

flexibility, *n.*   The state of being flexible.

FOB (free on board), *n.*   A point to which the transportation costs are borne by the seller and at which the title passes to the buyer.

to get in on the ground floor, *v.*   To get into a business or market early on so as to take advantage of its growth potential from the beginning.

hardball, softball, *adj.*   Describing two approaches to negotiations. *Hardball* suggests inflexibility, or trying to force the opposition to accept your conditions, while *softball* suggests a more flexible approach in which you try to reach an acceptable compromise.

to have connections, *v.*   To have people who can help you. In this case, these connections would be people in business.

inflexible, *adj.*   Unwilling to negotiate.

inflexibility, *n.*   The state of being rigid or inflexible.

negotiations, *n.* (**to negotiate,** *v.*)   The process of bargaining in an attempt to reach a mutually satisfying agreement or contract.

objectives, *n.*   Your goals; in this case, what you hope to obtain.

priority, *n.*   How you rate something in terms of its importance (high, medium, or low).

proposal, *n.* (**to propose,** *v.*)   What you offer as a basis for contract negotiations; often followed by a **counterproposal**, *n.* which is the other side's proposal in response to yours.

renegotiations, *n.* (**to renegotiate,** *v.*)   Negotiations carried out when a contract is renewed.

sanctions, *n.*   Penalties that can be imposed on the other side if they fail to accept your position.

to shy away, *v.*   To avoid.

strategy, *n.*   The plan you have for achieving your goals.

trading cards/tradables, *n.*   Demands that you are willing to give up in trade for some of your other demands.

traits, *n.*   Characteristics.

ultimatum, *n.*   A final proposal or terms whose rejection will result in the breaking off of negotiations.

unyielding, *adj.*   Refusing to compromise.

Midland Heating and Cooling vs. The Primary Sheet Metal Workers of America, AFL-CIO

CULTURAL BACKGROUND: UNION-MANAGEMENT RELATIONS

See the discussion of characteristics of American negotiation in the case Long-range Golf Equipment Seeks a Distributor (Case 4). The negotiations in this case may be even harder as, traditionally, union-management negotiations are quite tough. Try to put yourself in the mind frame of the negotiators, imagining how they would think and react, and carry out the negotiations as they would be performed in the United States. Remember, the *paternalistic* system of some countries, in which workers are guaranteed a job for life and a number of fringe benefits and thus feel loyalty to the company, does not exist in the United States. Thus, negotiations are much harder. Workers often feel that they are fighting for their livelihood because they believe that jobs are being lost to developing third-world countries.

CASE

This case involves negotiations between management and union representatives. In this case, the Primary Sheet Metal Workers Union will represent union shop workers in wage negotiations. The case allows you to practice English in a competitive negotiation situation. The negotiation has been simplified to allow you to solve the case within a reasonable time frame. In actuality, wage negotiations are more complex and are influenced by labor legislation, which varies from country to country. Still, an effort has been made to present a realistic case here, given the limitations of time. This case will be solved within an American framework because creating a case fitting all political systems would be impossible.

Negotiations require a certain amount of secrecy. The material given here is restricted to information that would be common knowledge to both sides. Position papers, which are secret, will be provided to both sides by the instructor. They will form the point of departure for your negotiation strategy. Do not allow them to be seen by members of the opposing group.

Midland Heating and Cooling

Midland Heating and Cooling was founded in 1954 by William and Robert Carothers. Their primary product is industrial heating and cooling units, and their primary customers are companies with large factories. The company is located in Toledo, Ohio, and employs 850 workers, which is approximately one-half of the work force employed during the company's peak years in the middle 1970s. As recently as 1986, Midland employed 1,250 workers, but downsizing and the recession have taken their toll on the work force. The streamlining undertaken in the 1980s allowed Midland to remain profitable, and the income statements from the last three years reflect this:

Year	Sales	Net Profit after Taxes	Return on Sales (%)	Market Share (%)
1994	$55,890,000	$5,600,000	10.2	2.25
1993	63,976,000	6,100,000	9.6	2.34
1992	66,450,000	6,150,000	9.3	2.50

Despite falling sales, return on sales is improving. The union claims that the increased productivity of the workers, up 10 percent over the last three years, is the cause of the increased return on sales. Although encouraged by this trend, management is concerned about the falling market share that can only be reversed by keeping salary raises moderate. However, the union is quick to point out that wages over the past contract period of three years have kept up with neither inflation nor the industry's average, citing these figures:

Inflation for the past three years:	12 percent (4 percent per year)
Salary increases at Midland for the past three years:	10 percent
Salary increases for the industry for the past three years:	12 percent

Management claims that their workers *are* getting higher salaries if one looks at the salaries and benefit package as a whole, because the cost of health insurance has gone up 34 percent over the past three years. Management has hinted that they may have to drop health insurance coverage for their workers if costs continue to rise. At present, it costs Midland $3,000 per year to insure each worker and his or her family. Furthermore, management estimates for the present year show a 10 percent decline in sales due to the recession, which means the company must cut costs in order to maintain its market share. Naturally, the workers will be expected to carry their share of the burden to allow Midland to remain competitive. There is no immediate threat of Midland going bankrupt since their equity level is a respectable 30 percent, but management is concerned about the effects of the recession and the company's declining market share.

POINTS FOR DISCUSSION

Discuss how wages and working conditions are determined in your country, and compare this method with the union versus management approach described in this case. Do you have a union and management system? If not, what system is used to determine wages and working conditions? If so:

a. What are typical demands from workers? Are strikes used as sanctions?

b. Is the relationship between unions and management confrontational or cooperative?

CASE ACTIVITIES

Negotiating a Union-Management Agreement

You will be negotiating the package for the factory workers, with one group acting as management representatives, the other as union representatives. All the workers are represented by the Primary Sheet Metal Workers of America, AFL-CIO (the leading federation of unions in the United States). At present, the average salary for journeymen is $10.15 an hour based on seniority. There is only one shift, so there will be no question of shift differential. It has been standard practice in these negotiations to set an across-the-board percentage increase for each of the three years in a contract period. There is nothing that says that you cannot negotiate a one-year contract, but this has not been the practice in the past.

At present, the workers have the following benefits:

1. Health care insurance (major medical) for the worker and all family members living with him or her up to the age of 18.

2. A pension plan based on an equal sharing of the cost between management and the workers.

3. Paid holidays beginning with two weeks the first four years and three weeks after that.

4. Additional paid national holidays.

5. A clothing allowance for work clothes.

6. Time and a half for overtime over forty hours per week.

The workers have recently expressed concern over rumors that Midland intends to subcontract some of the work, and management knows this will be an issue. In addition, the union is against hiring part-time workers because that can lead to layoffs. Management cites the rising cost of health care as one reason for wanting to hire part-time workers, as these workers do not have to be covered by health care insurance. In these times of rising unemployment, the workers want a no-layoff guarantee and *job posting*. Job posting refers to the announcing of all jobs through the local union and internal promotion. COLAs (cost of living adjustments) are a standard union demand. COLAs mean that the workers will be compensated for inflation so that wage increases will represent real increases in buying power, thereby counteracting the trend in which the workers actually suffered a 2 percent decrease in buying power over the last three-year period. Naturally, management is against COLAs because they increase costs, making the estimation of future costs difficult; this, in turn, complicates the company's ability to bid successfully on contracts.

After each team has prepared its negotiation strategy (by filling out a negotiations worksheet like the one in Case 4, Long-range Golf Equipment Seeks a Distributor), they will meet at the negotiation table to try to work out a contract. The following questions will be considered:

1. Wages
2. Cost of living adjustments (COLAs)
3. A no-layoff guarantee
4. Part-time work
5. Subcontracting (buying certain parts or products from an outside producer instead of producing them, which would mean loss of jobs at Midland)
6. Job posting

After the teams have worked out a contract, they will present the result orally to the class. During the oral presentation, the team representatives will discuss their individual strategies and how successful they were in achieving their goals. They will explain why they agreed to the concessions they made and what they obtained in return for these concessions. There will be as many negotiations as there are teams (naturally, two teams per negotiation).

LANGUAGE MASTERY EXERCISE

Practicing Common Negotiation Phrases and Techniques

Negotiating involves the use of certain phrases to help master the process. Learn the following phrases, which you will use in your negotiations.

CHECKING THAT YOU HAVE UNDERSTOOD:

Please correct me if I'm wrong, but . . .

Could I ask a few questions to see whether I have understood your position?

Could we go through that again?

SHOWING WILLINGNESS TO COOPERATE:

We would like to settle this issue in a mutually satisfactory way.

We'd be happy to settle this point in a mutually cooperative way.

PROPOSING A SOLUTION TO REACH A COMPROMISE:

What if we were to . . . ?

Supposing we tried . . . ?

Wouldn't a fair solution be . . . ?

SHOWING UNDERSTANDING:

> We appreciate your problem, but . . .
>
> We can understand your difficulty, but . . .

FOCUSING ON DIFFICULTIES:

> The main problem as we see it is . . .
>
> Where we have difficulty with your proposal is . . .

REJECTING AN OFFER:

> I'm afraid we won't be able to accept that [*diplomatic*].
>
> I'm afraid that you are going to have to meet our requests on this item if we are going to reach an agreement.
>
> That is totally out of the question [*strong*].

ACCEPTING AN OFFER:

> I think we can accept that.
>
> I think we can agree on that.

VOCABULARY

across-the-board increase, *n.*   A wage increase given to all or nearly all employees at one time. This is in the form of a percentage or dollar-and-cents increase, such as 5 percent or $0.50 per hour.

agreement, *n.*   A contract or mutual understanding between a union and a company setting forth the terms and conditions of employment, such as salaries, benefits, and other working conditions.

apprentice, *n.*   One who is learning a trade or craft and who receives lower wages than a journeyman.

arbitration (American), *n.*   A situation in which parties unable to agree on a contract have submitted the final decision to a third party.

attrition, (British: **natural wastage**), *n.*   Reducing the work force through retirement, not layoffs.

bargaining, *n.*   Negotiating a contract (in this case, a contract to set forth the conditions of employment).

bottom line, *n.*   In this case, as far as you are willing to go to meet the other party to reach an agreement.

COLAs (cost of living adjustments), *n.*   Compensation for inflation so that wage increases represent real wage increases. This is a common union demand, but at present, COLAs are rarely awarded by management.

collective bargaining, *n.*   A process in which representatives from the union and management work out a contract specifying the conditions of employment.

counter-proposal, *n.*   An offer made in response to an offer made by the other party in negotiations.

deadlocked, *adj.*   When negotiations reach an **impasse**, meaning that no further progress can be made; this generally means that the decision must be turned over to an arbitrator.

downsizing, *n.*   Reducing the size of a company's workforce.

earnings, *n.*   The amount of money received by a worker, including salary, bonuses, commissions, overtime pay, and so on.

to employ, *v.*   To hire.

employee, *n.*   Anyone who works for an employer.

employer, *n.*   A person, association, or company having workers in its employ.

equity, *n.*   Real assets (all things owned by a business and having some money value).

grievance, *n.*   Any complaint by an employee or by a union about any aspect of employment.

health insurance, *n.*   As the United States does not have national health insurance, unions must negotiate to obtain health insurance coverage for their workers.

journeyman, *n.*   A worker in a craft or trade who has served an apprenticeship and is qualified for employment at the journeyman's rate of pay.

layoff, *n.*   Temporary or indefinite termination of employment, usually due to a lack of work. This is not the same as discharge (firing).

lockout, *n.*   When unions refuse to accept an employer's conditions, the employer can close the factory to the present employees and even hire new employees. This is the employer's sanction, which corresponds to the union's sanction of a strike.

market share, *n.*   The percentage of the total market that a product has.

mediation, *n.*   A situation in which a neutral person, or **mediator**, works with labor and management to help them reach an agreement.

musts, *n.*   Important demands that you must get if you are going to accept an agreement.

negotiations, *n.*   Discussion with the intent of reaching an agreement.

picketing, *n.*   The act of patrolling at or near the employer's place of business during a strike to inform the public that there is a labor dispute in progress or to prevent strike breakers from entering the place of employment. **Picket,** *n.* One who does the picketing.

productivity, *n.*   An index to measure the efficiency of a plant in utilizing its work force and equipment.

raise, (British: **rise**), *n.*   An increase in wages.

ratification, *n.*   The acceptance by the members of a union of a contract worked out between the representatives of the union and management.

real wages, *n.*   The real worth of one's wages (present and future) in terms of buying power, which is affected by inflation.

recession, *n.*   A temporary decline in business activity.

seniority, *n.*   The length of time an employee has worked at a company. Seniority is frequently a factor in determining promotions and layoffs.

shift, *n.*   The set period of time one works, such as 8:00 A.M. to 4:00 P.M.

shift differential, *n.*   Different rates of pay for different shifts.

shop steward, *n.*   The representative of the union at the place of work.

strike, *n.*   A work stoppage on the part of the employees to force management to meet the union's demands.

strikebreakers, *n.*   Employees hired while the original work force is on strike so that the company can continue its operations; also called **scabs** (a derogatory expression).

strike fund, *n.*   The amount of money a union has to support its workers while they are on strike.

to subcontract, *v.*   To buy certain parts or items from another producer.

trading cards, *n.*   Demands that you are willing to trade away in order to get your most important demands — that is, your "musts."

wage, *n.*   The price paid by the employer for work or services rendered by an employee.

wage cut, *n.*   A reduction in wages.

work day, *n.*   The time spent by an employee at work during a normal day, usually eight hours.

ENVIRONMENT AND BUSINESS LEADERS' SOCIAL RESPONSIBILITY

Northern Electrical Services vs. the Environmentalists

CULTURAL BACKGROUND: ENVIRONMENTAL GROUPS

Due to increased concern for the fate of our planet, environmental groups have become both more popular and stronger. There are a number of groups, such as the Sierra Club and Greenpeace, which, through demonstrations and lobbying (providing information to politicians in the hope of influencing the way they vote), have begun to have a strong impact both on people's awareness of the dangers of increased pollution and on political decisions. Organizations like these have local groups that monitor local conditions. Political activism at the local level is typical in the United States, as people's loyalties are strongly connected to their local environment. On the other hand, Americans tend to feel just as strongly that the individual should decide his or her own fate, and that feeling carries over to companies in a free-enterprise system, prompting a dislike of regulations. Because many environmental regulations in the United States are determined by the federal (national) government, it is not uncommon for local residents to react against them, especially if the loss of jobs is a result of the regulations. Thus, this case brings out the conflicts between local loyalties, dislike of federal regulation, and fear of loss of jobs. Americans would be very emotional in a meeting such as the one in this case and would express their feelings freely.

CASE

This case deals with one of the basic questions that most business leaders will face eventually: environmental responsibility. Industrial waste, though not the only source of pollution, has been a focus of environmental groups, such as the Sierra Club and Greenpeace, with a special emphasis on waste dumping and air pollution. It has been claimed that business leaders have frequently avoided their environmental responsibilities by pretending not to know about their company's emissions or claiming that expenses associated with cleanups and factory modernization would be prohibitively expensive. When faced with demands from environmental groups and governmental agencies, business leaders sometimes threaten plant closures. The effect may be that the local population, fearing unemployment, turns on environmental groups. Politicians, fearing defeat in the next election, may decide not to pressure businesses to pollute less.

However, according to World Watch, an environmental organization, if we do not seriously reduce pollutants being released into the atmosphere within forty years, we will face an environmental catastrophe. One possible scenario is that global warming, due to the greenhouse effect, will lead to mass flooding of low-lying areas and a radical increase in the total desert area. Another problem is the thinning of the ozone layer due to CFC (chlorofluorocarbons) gases, which will lead to a dramatic rise in the number of skin cancer cases.

POINTS FOR DISCUSSION

1. In your country, are industrial leaders fully aware of the amount of pollution their companies emit into the environment? If yes, what are they doing to reduce it? If not, why not? Is it because they don't want to accept the responsibility and costs associated with such pollution, or is it due to a lack of information?
2. Should industrial leaders be more responsive to the problem of pollution? What can be done, if necessary, to make them responsive?
3. What sanctions (such as fines, jail sentences, and so on) would be most effective in cases of repeated environmental offenses on the part of local industries?

CASE ACTIVITIES

A Public Hearing

Many companies' environmental records are being investigated. Such is the case with Northern Electrical Services. This company is located in a town of 12,000 people along the Connecticut River in Connecticut. It employs 800 people and is the town's largest employer in an area with over 10 percent unemployment. If the company were to close operations, it would be an economic disaster for the community. Not only would the unemployment figures double immediately, but the effect on local businesses would threaten the entire economic base of the community.

Northern Electrical Services services parts for electrical power plants. PCBs, a toxic material, were once used in producing many of the components the company services, and tests done by local environmentalists show that a ten-mile down-river stretch of the Connecticut River has high concentrations of PCBs in the river sediments. In addition, PCB concentrations in fish caught in the river are twice the FDA (Food and Drug Administration) standards of two ppm (parts per million) for levels of PCBs in fish. The number of cancer patients in the local area is 50 percent higher than the national average. In addition, the number of spontaneous abortions in the local area is 40 percent higher than the national average. Although there is no definite proof that the PCBs in the river sediments are the direct cause of these high rates of illness, it is difficult to find any other explanation. In any case, the possibility of a health risk has limited the use of the most important recreational area the townspeople have — the Connecticut River.

Another major problem allegedly caused by Northern Electrical Services is the emission of sulfur dioxide and nitrogen oxide from their heating unit, which burns fossil fuels (oil, gas, and coal). The company's plant, which was constructed in 1945, has inadequate cleansing equipment in its smoke stacks. The management has estimated that the installation of the most advanced filters would cost $2 million dollars, which is approximately half of the company's annual profits. It is estimated that this equipment would eliminate 99 percent of all sulfur dioxide and nitrogen oxide, which would greatly improve the air quality in the area. As it is now, poor air quality is blamed for nausea, headaches, and a high rate of respiratory diseases in the area. Forty percent of all school-age children suffer from asthma. Northern Electrical Services, on the other hand, claims that their sulfur dioxide and nitrogen oxide emissions are within the EPA (Environmental Protection Agency) limits of 1.2 pounds per million BTUs and 0.6 pounds per million BTUs respectively. Thus, they feel that they are adhering to the law and do not feel any responsibility to install new filters. An opinion poll taken in a local newspaper found that 62 percent of the population felt that Northern Electrical Services had a responsibility to install the new filters; 28 percent felt that emission controls were adequate, while 10 percent had no opinion.

In terms of responsibility, the local environmentalist organization's representative wrote a letter to the editor of the local newspaper stating that Northern Electrical Services should be held responsible for cleaning up the entire stretch of the Connecticut River polluted with PCBs — a process that would cost an estimated $25 million dollars. Naturally, the company's spokesperson responded that this demand was unrealistic, since it would force the closing of the plant. The plant is not highly profitable as it is, and even the cost of installing smokestack equipment could push the administration to consider closing the plant.

The local environmentalists further demand a study of health conditions of the workers at Northern Electrical Services paid for by the company. Its purpose would be both to help improve the possibility of limiting the number of deaths from cancer through early detection, and to determine if workers at the factory are more prone to develop cancer. If this was the case, the environmentalists would bring a *class-action suit* (a lawsuit representing the interests of a group of people) on behalf of the workers.

With the obvious conflicts of interest and strong emotions, tempers have been flying. In a few cases, the tension has led to violent confrontations between workers, who are afraid of losing their jobs, and environmentalists. Thus, the mayor of the town has called a hearing. She has invited representatives from the management of Northern Electrical Services, the environmentalists, the factory workers, and representatives of the State Department of Environmental Protection. In addition, all residents of the town are welcome to attend. Each group participating in the meeting will have to prepare its role separately, and then come to the meeting with carefully prepared positions and arguments.

Management of Northern Electrical Services

You will try to present your company in the best light, talking about your civic concern and showing what you have done for the community and what your business means for the local economy. You will present a study that confirms that your emissions of sulfur dioxide and nitrogen oxide are within the EPA limits stated above. You will also emphasize that there is no proof that the PCBs stem from your factory. You will explain the financial situation of your company and the limitations that situation puts on meeting the demands raised by the environmentalists.

You must work out a position much like that needed for other negotiation cases in this book (see Cases 4 and 5). Determine how far you are willing to go to meet environmentalists' expected demands and where your bottom line is. What is your attitude going to be? Will you deny all responsibility and threaten to close the plant, or are you willing to make some concessions? You should keep in mind that if it is proven that you have exceeded EPA limits for sulfur dioxide and nitrogen oxide emissions, you may be charged fines levied by the Connecticut State Department of Environmental Protection, which has the final authority in this case. Your team will consist of representatives from management, plus your highly paid lawyers.

The Workers

You have two conflicting concerns. Your major concern is the possible loss of your jobs, and thus you basically are aligned with management and against the environmentalists. However, you are also concerned about your health and the health of your family. Information about the high incidence of cancer and respiratory diseases in your community concerns you and will affect what you say in the meeting.

The Environmentalists

Naturally, you are the most outspoken group. You will come to the meeting armed with statistics, charts, and a list of demands. Your statistics will present a different picture than that of the management of Northern Electrical Services. You will try to enlist the support of the local residents.

Local Residents

You share similar concerns with the workers; that is, you are concerned with both the economic and the health aspects of the case. You are free to express individual opinions or formulate a unified position for your entire group.

The Connecticut State Department of Environmental Protection

Your group consists of four to five members of the department. You will listen to arguments from all participants and formulate a judgment. If you find that Northern Electrical Services has broken the law, you can force them to take necessary steps to bring air pollution within EPA standards. You can even force them to clean up the down-river stretch of the Connecticut River if it is proven that they are the sole, or major, polluter. You can also levy fines. One of your members will chair the meeting. (See Meeting Terminology and Procedures in Case 3.)

Each group will prepare individually, and then come to the town meeting well prepared.

The Meeting

The chairperson will call the meeting to order. The management from Northern Electrical Services will be allowed to present their case at the front of the room. After they are finished, the environmentalists will be allowed to present their case and their demands at the front of the room. Then the discussion will be opened to the floor, which means that anyone can speak, either as a representative of a group or as a person expressing an individual opinion. The representatives of the management and the environmentalists will remain in front of the class to answer any questions or respond to any comments.

After the chairperson feels that the positions have been adequately presented, he or she will adjourn the meeting and set a date for a follow-up meeting. In the follow-up meeting, the representatives of the State Department of Environmental Management will present their decision, beginning by announcing whether or not Northern Electrical Services has broken the law. If the Department representatives determine that Northern Electrical Services *has* broken the law, they must announce which specific points the company is responsible for, and what they must do to remedy the situation. Also, Department representatives must determine whether any fines are going to be levied, and if so, how much the company will be charged.

LANGUAGE MASTERY EXERCISES

Presenting an Opinion and Responding to Others' Opinions

In debating questions such as the one in this case, you will have to (1) present an opinion, and (2) agree and/or disagree with others' opinions. Below you will find expressions commonly used in this kind of situation, followed by an exercise in using these expressions.

PRESENTING AN OPINION

It seems to me . . . *or* It appears to me . . . [*weak*]
I feel that . . . *or* I think that . . . *or* It is my opinion that . . . [*neutral*]
I am convinced that . . . *or* I strongly/firmly believe that . . . [*strong*]
There is no question/doubt that . . . [*very strong*]

GETTING ANOTHER PERSON'S OPINION

Mr. Smith, I would like your opinion/input on this matter.
Mr. Smith, what do you think/feel about this matter?

RESPONDING

Agreeing
I generally agree . . . [*agreement, but with reservations*]
I agree . . . [*neutral*]
I fully/completely agree . . . [*strong*]

Disagreeing

I'm afraid that I cannot agree . . . [*polite disagreement*]

I can see your point, but . . . [*polite disagreement*]

I cannot totally agree . . . [*partial disagreement*]

I cannot completely agree . . . [*partial disagreement*]

I strongly/totally disagree . . . [*strong*]

Verbal Exercise

One student should express an opinion and then, using the above phrases, the other students should in turn express agreement or disagreement and state why. After three or four students have expressed their opinions about the original opinion or any of the other students' responses, have a new student express a new opinion and get other students' responses.

WRITING: EXPRESSING YOUR OPINION

1. Write a letter to the local newspaper expressing your point of view on this case. (This exercise is for all groups except the Connecticut State Department of Environmental Protection group.)

2. The Connecticut State Department of Environmental Protection group will write a report summarizing (a) the information presented at the meeting, and (b) their decision in the case, supported by the facts presented in the course of the meeting.

VOCABULARY

abatement, *n.*   Reducing the amount of, or eliminating, pollution.

air pollutant, *n.*   Any substance in the air which could, in high enough concentration, harm human beings, other animals, vegetation, or other material.

air pollution, *n.*   The presence of air pollutants that have a harmful effect on human beings, animals, vegetation, or other material.

to align, *v.*   To be on the same side as someone else.

biodegradable, *adj.*   Able to break down or decompose rapidly under natural conditions and processes.

carbon dioxide (CO$_2$), *n.*   A colorless, odorless, nonpoisonous gas which results from burning fossil fuels. Carbon dioxide is a major contributor to smog and the greenhouse effect.

carcinogenic, *adj.*   Cancer-producing.

chlorofluorocarbons (CFC), *n.*   Gases that deplete the ozone layer.

class-action suit, *n.*   A law suit brought on behalf of a group of people.

cleanup, *n.*   Actions taken to clean up a polluted area (in this case, dredging the river to remove sediments containing PCBs).

desulfurization, *n.*   The removal of sulfur from fossil fuels to reduce pollution. Desulfurization is a process that, along with filtering or scrubbing, can significantly reduce the amount of air pollution from factories like the one in this case.

dredging, *n.*   The removal of mud from the bottom of water bodies, using a machine. Dredging might be necessary to remove the PCBs in the sediments of the river in this case. But dredging can also produce negative side effects such as silting, which can kill life in the river.

effluent, *n.*   Waste water that flows into bodies of water.

emission, *n.*   Pollution discharged into the atmosphere from smokestacks and the like. The nitrogen oxide and sulfur dioxide emitted by the factory in this case are emissions.

emission standard, *n.*   The maximum amount of air-polluting discharge legally allowed from a single source.

enforcement, *n.*   The action of forcing companies to obey laws (in this case, environmental laws like the Clean Water and Clean Air Acts).

to enlist, *n.*   To seek the support of.

EPA, *n.*   The U.S. Environmental Protection Agency is the government agency charged with enforcing environmental legislation.

to exceed, *v.*   To emit more pollution than allowed by environmental legislation.

greenhouse effect, *n.*   The warming of the earth's atmosphere caused by a buildup of carbon dioxide or other gases. It is believed by many scientists that this buildup allows light from the sun's rays to heat the earth but prevents the escape of heat from the earth's atmosphere.

to levy, *v.*   To demand payment.

to monitor, *v.*   To check regularly.

National Ambient Air Quality Standards (NAAQS), *n.*   Air quality standards established by the EPA.

National Emission Standards for Hazardous Air Pollutants (NESHAPs), *n.*   Emission standards set by the EPA for air pollutants not covered by NAAQS.

nitrogen oxide, (NOX), *n.*   Gases produced in fossil fuel combustion.

ozone (O_3), *n.*   A gas found in two layers of the atmosphere, the stratosphere and the troposphere. In the stratosphere (the atmospheric layer beginning seven to ten miles above the earth's surface), ozone forms a protective shield protecting the earth from ultraviolet radiation which, in too large doses, causes skin cancer. This layer is rapidly being depleted by CFC gases.

PCBs, *n.*   A group of toxic chemicals used in transformers and capacitators for insulating purposes. Further sale or new use of PCBs was banned by law in 1979.

pollutant, *n.*   Any substance introduced into the environment that produces undesired environmental effects.

pollution, *n.*   The presence of matter or energy whose nature, location, or quantity produces undesired environmental effects.

sediments, *n.*   Soil, sand, and minerals washed from land into water. In this case, sediments could have carried PCBs into the riverbed, where fish feeding on the bottom would have ingested them.

sulfur dioxide (SO_2), *n.*   A heavy, pungent gas produced by industrial fossil fuel combustion.

BUSINESS

ORGANIZATION

AND MANAGEMENT

Commutair:
Employee Motivation
and Management Theory

CULTURAL BACKGROUND: WORK FORCE MOTIVATION

This case reflects various aspects of British culture, where there is a democratic tradition in which employees are used to fighting for their rights and managers are aware of the importance of motivation in a service-sector company. In cultures like that in Great Britain, which tend to emphasize the individual, there is a tendency to try to motivate the work force to perform better. In cultures in which there is a strong loyalty to one's company, there is not the same emphasis on motivational theory, as motivation is built into the employees' attitude toward the company and the company's expectations of the employees. In these cultures, employees are expected to work hard because of their loyalty to the company, while in cultures that stress individualism, the employees must be motivated to work hard.

Thus, motivational strategies are considered an important part of the activities of the human resources (also called personnel) department within cultures that emphasize the individual.

CASE

Commutair, a small commuter airline based in Newcastle in the United Kingdom, has flights between Newcastle, Aberdeen, and Edinburgh, as well as flights from these cities to London. The airline has recently applied for concessions for routes from the three northern cities to Oslo and Bergen (Norway), Gothenburg (Sweden), and Aarhus (Denmark). However, recent developments have begun to create uneasiness in the company. Judging from an increased number of customer complaints, there seems to be growing customer dissatisfaction. The complaints center around lost baggage, overbooking, delayed flights, inadequate information to passengers, and impoliteness. The president of the company, Tom Waters, fears that some of these problems can be tied to employee dissatisfaction. In addition, absenteeism is increasing, which supports management's fears of growing employee discontent. A brief survey of employee opinion has revealed dissatisfaction with pay (which is 10 percent under the industry average), the monotony of work (especially at the check-in counter), and frustration with managers who are not willing to listen to suggestions and complaints from "front-line" employees in response to customer demands and complaints.

Waters has followed up the survey with interviews, receiving the following responses. John Jacobs, a baggage handler, complained about eight-hour shifts with no coffee room in which to take a break, as well as problems with the electric baggage trucks which result in breakdowns and the need to reload the baggage onto new trucks. Margaret McKinney, a flight attendant, reported constant customer complaints (including a lack of snacks in tourist class and the absence of newspapers in business class) to her manager four months ago and has still received no reply. The check-in personnel are frustrated with reservation personnel for constant overbooking and have continually complained to their manager. One check-in employee, Jennifer Roberts, said that if the situation was not remedied soon, she would quit. She cannot stand the constant complaints she is getting, particularly since it does not appear as if anything will be done about the situation. Reservation personnel are also frustrated, as they receive constant complaints from the check-in personnel without being able to do anything about company policy concerning overbooking. (The reservations manager has insisted that overbooking is necessary to insure that flights are full, despite last-minute cancellations.)

Company President Waters is afraid that the application for new routes will be jeopardized if something is not done soon to reverse the rise in employee — and customer — dissatisfaction. He has asked the Director of Human Resources to set up a committee, consisting of members of her staff and other employees, to discuss the present situation and write a report suggesting necessary changes. As members of this committee, you must consider the major complaints of the employees, as well as possible changes the administration must make to meet these demands. Basically, you are being asked to consider what motivates front-line employees in an airline in general, and what must be done specifically in response to Commutair employees' complaints. How can the front-line employees be motivated to be more service-minded? Finally, what changes in management philosophy and organizational structure must be made to meet employee needs?

POINTS FOR DISCUSSION

1. Compare the attitude of people within your culture toward work and the necessity for motivation with the situation in this case. Are your workers naturally motivated as a result of respect for, and loyalty to, the management and the company? If not, what are the typical means used by management to motivate workers?
2. How important is a knowledge of motivation theory for managers?
3. How much motivation theory have you learned in your studies or on the job?
4. Discuss what would best motivate employees in a company such as Commutair. Is money or job satisfaction the most important issue?

CASE ACTIVITIES

Management/Employee Discussions

Each group will function as a separate committee. Each committee will consist of (a) front-line employees with specific demands and (b) members of the Human Resources Department who possess a good knowledge of motivation and management theory. The employees on the committee should represent specific employee groups, such as check-in, baggage, cabin, and reservations personnel. You should begin by discussing what motivates personnel in front-line jobs such as yours. You can discuss this in general, using motivation theory, and then talk about what would motivate you in your specific job.

The next step will be to discuss managerial theories and approaches that management should adopt to meet the employees' demands. Here you will have to step out of your roles as employees and look at the problem from the point of view of consultants trying to consider the needs of both management and employees. You should discuss managerial theories relevant to a service company and devise a managerial policy statement for Commutair. This statement should include (1) a statement of management's attitude toward their employees, (2) a motivational package to meet the needs of the employees, and (3) changes in organizational structure to increase communication and give front-line employees more say in company policy. In addition, it should include a statement about the importance of a customer- and service-oriented attitude among the employees. The statement of policy should be illustrated with concrete examples of how this policy and attitude will be implemented in the future. (See the Vocabulary list on pages 66–67 for more ideas concerning motivation).

The Meeting

This case will be carried out as a committee meeting and an open discussion of the points mentioned above. The results of the meeting will be reported to the class and also written up in the form of a report to be handed in. Your oral and written reports will cover the following areas:

1. A managerial policy statement concerning management's attitude toward the employees.
2. A motivational package offered to the employees to help meet their demands. This package might include pay raises, profit sharing, better shifts, job rotation, more influence on decision making, and so on.
3. Proposed changes in the organizational structure to meet employee demands (see the present organizational chart shown in Figure 7-1).
4. A statement of a customer- and service-oriented policy expected to be followed by all levels of employees.

Tips in Solving This Case

In preparing this case, consider the following success stories in the airline industry.

1. **Donald Burr, People Express.** Although now defunct, People Express was extremely successful for a brief period of time, and Donald Burr was famous industry-wide as a motivational genius. Even though his company went bankrupt (due to overexpansion) and his ideas proved to be less successful near the end, they could be useful in formulating a motivational package. (See Harvard Business School Case 483-103, "People Express.")

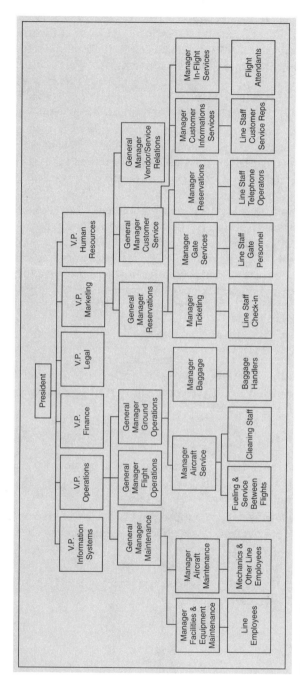

Figure 7-1   Organizational Chart: Commutair

2. **Jane Carlzon, SAS.** Carlzon has been very successful as head of SAS. Even more important for you, he has written and spoken extensively on the subject of employee motivation and managerial theory. (See Jan Carlzon, *Moments of Truth*, Cambridge, Mass.: Ballinger Publishing Co., 1987.)

3. **Alaska Airlines** is one of the few U.S. airlines enjoying economic success. Like Commutair, it is a small airline and bears watching. See recent articles.

4. **Harvard Business School Case 575-118,** "Southwest Airlines," analyzes another successful small airline.

Harvard Business School Case 9-482-017, "Note on Rewards Systems," gives a good overview of successful management/motivational strategies. Other sources of information are standard textbooks in Organization and Management. All Harvard Business School cases can be obtained from Harvard Business School Case Services, Harvard School of Business, Boston, MA 02163, USA.

LANGUAGE MASTERY EXERCISE

Word Choice and Attitudes

A positive attitude is important in business, and your choice of words is vital in creating the right attitude. Compare the statement "Our jobs are boring" with the statement "Our jobs could be more stimulating and our performance better if. . . ." The first statement is negative and reflects a passivity, whereas the second one is positive and reflects a desire to improve the situation.

Working in pairs, take the following sentences related to this case and create more positive statements either by using the hints as starters or by making your own entirely new sentences.

1. There is no communication between front-line employees and the decision makers.

    Hint: Better communication between front-line employees and decision makers would . . .

2. Management doesn't have a personnel policy that considers our needs.

    Hint: Work motivation would be improved if . . .

3. There are too many levels in our present organizational structure.

    Hint: We could respond better to customers' needs if . . .

4. We have no say in the running of our company.

    Hint: If we could have more say in the running of our company, . . .

5. The monotony in our jobs is unbearable.

    Hint: We would be . . . if . . .

6. Our salaries are far too low.

    Hint: We would be more . . . if . . .

7. Our company has no personnel policy.

    Hint: Perhaps our job performance would . . . if . . .

WRITING: MEETING REPORT

Each group should hand in the report described previously in "The Meeting" section.

VOCABULARY

absenteeism, *n.*   The number of workers absent from work.

to assess, *v.*   To observe and evaluate someone's job performance.

behavior modification, *n.*   A technique that aims at changing an employee's behavior in a desired direction.

compensation, *n.*   A reward or payment for services.

to evaluate, *v.*   To rate a person's job performance.

evaluation, *n.*   The rating of a person's job performance. Synonym: **assessment,** *n.*

fringe benefits, *n.*   Any rewards given to an employee in addition to salary, such as a company car, an expense account, a free home phone, and so on. Synonym: **perk,** *n.* (considered slang by some people, but often used).

gratification, *n.*   Satisfaction of a need.

incentive, *n.*   Something that stimulates performance, such as a **bonus** (additional monetary compensation), **profit sharing** (sharing a percentage of the profits with the employees), or **stock options** (allowing employees to buy shares in the company at a favorable price).

to implement, *v.*   To put into practice.

job design, *n.*   The way job tasks are structured and carried out, including the following options:

job enrichment, *n.*   Tailoring job tasks so that work is more satisfying for the employees.

flextime, *n.*   Allowing employees to determine their work schedules within certain latitudes.

4/40, *n.*   A work week made up of four 10-hour days.

quality control circles, *n.*   A group of employees with similar tasks and responsibilities who meet regularly to discuss how they can improve job performance and products.

job rotation, *n.*   A system that provides an employee a variety of tasks to reduce monotony and boredom.

merit-based compensation plan, *n.*   Salary based primarily on an employee's performance.

motivation, *n.*   Something that encourages or drives a person to act in a desired way.

performance, *n.* The way an employee carries out his or her job.

promotion, *n.* Raising an employee to a higher position in the company.

to promote, *v.* To raise an employee to a higher position.

raise, *n.* An increase in salary.

recognition, *n.* Public acknowledgment of a good job performance.

reinforcement, *n.* Something that causes certain behavior to be repeated or inhibited. **Positive reinforcement** encourages a desired behavior; **negative reinforcement** discourages undesired behavior.

reward, *n.* A token given in recognition of good job performance.

to reward, *v.* To provide a token in recognition of good job performance.

BUSINESS

ORGANIZATION

AND MANAGEMENT

Unhealthy Leaders:
Sterling Forklift

CULTURAL BACKGROUND: ANGLO/AMERICAN MANAGEMENT STYLES

This case, like Case 7 on Commutair, emphasizes the importance of creating an atmosphere in which employees are encouraged to perform at their best. In many cultures, bosses are so highly respected that their management style would not be questioned. However, in Anglo/American cultures, this is not the case. In this case, the employees of the British company Sterling Forklift consider the managerial style of their company's president so destructive of good working conditions that they feel obliged to confront him. The relatively open nature of British society allows for conflict between employees and their employer. The British have a long tradition of class conflict and confrontation between unions and management. Management has not always been responsive to workers' needs and, as in this case, must sometimes be forced to face these needs. Unlike managers in some other cultures, British managers are not so secure in their position that they cannot be confronted. Conflict is accepted as part of the relationship between workers and management, and British society allows for the conflict to be expressed.

CASE

In a recent Norwegian book about management style, the author states that managers' leadership styles can actually lead to health problems and high absenteeism among the employees. One of these unhealthy styles is exhibited by Tom Masters, the founder and president of Sterling Forklift. Thus, this case deals not just with reorganization, but also with human personalities and conflicts. No matter where people work, they are going to run into conflicts of ideas, personalities, and management styles. The ability of employees and managers to resolve these conflicts satisfactorily will affect not only their working environment, but also the company's overall performance.

This case involves conflicts between the Engineering and Production Departments of Sterling Forklift — conflicts that are intensified by Masters's pressure on employees. Due to the pressure they are under, the two heads of the departments could easily turn to blaming each other as a way of avoiding Masters's anger. Naturally, this would have a negative effect on the working environment at

Sterling Forklift, as well as on the working relationship between engineering and production.

Sterling Forklift of Sterling, Scotland, makes battery-powered forklifts. It has been expanding rapidly, as it has managed to position itself in a new market created by government regulation requiring a reduction of pollution in the workplace. The company is headed by Tom Masters, the founder of the company. He is a hardheaded engineer with an eye for figures and a corresponding lack of psychological insight into employee motivation. The original forklift model produced by Sterling Forklift was Masters's "baby," and although he has hired engineers to further its development, he is constantly "dropping by" and more or less dictating to them how to carry out their jobs. The Production Manager, James Dickerson, an Englishman, and the Engineering Manager, William McRoberts, a Scot, feel that Masters is constantly pressuring their workers. They are professionals and do not want to be treated like assembly-line workers. However, Masters cannot seem to make this distinction. Masters's management style is particularly troubling to McRoberts, who has a degree in engineering and an MBA. Besides Masters's impolite manner, his management style includes monthly meetings with the managers, in which the managers must account for the past month's performance. These meetings in Masters's office take on the character of calling the employees on the carpet (criticizing them). Masters has even yelled at McRoberts during several of these meetings and stated point-blank that if McRoberts cannot perform up to expectations, he should consider finding employment elsewhere. The two criteria Masters uses to measure the Engineering and the Production Departments' performances are (a) cost efficiency and (b) quality control. McRoberts's department has recently experienced Masters's anger due to their slowness in working out problems in a new model that is now three months behind schedule. On several of his visits to the Engineering Department, Masters has embarrassed McRoberts by criticizing him in front of his staff.

Dickerson has also experienced Masters's abrasive management style. Masters is a stickler for cost efficiency and quality control, and Production is not living up to his expectations, especially in the area of cost efficiency. Dickerson feels that Masters's criticism is unfair, as Dickerson has been calling for a reorganization of the assembly system from bays to an assembly-line. Masters refuses to listen to Dickerson, saying that the conversion of the factory would be too expensive in terms of both the cost of the conversion and lost production time. The conversion is estimated by Masters to cost £1.7 million, plus another £300,000 in carrying the cost of overheads during the conversion, as well as the costs of overtime pay to train workers on the new assembly-line and to build up inventory. Dickerson counters that this conversion would increase productivity by 20 percent, which would compensate for the cost in approximately three years (the new assembly-line is expected to generate a £670,000 incremental cash flow). However, Dickerson's argument has been ignored (see point 2, Power barriers, on page 72, for a possible explanation).

In addition, both Dickerson and McRoberts are beginning to sense discontent among their staff, and there has been talk about some of the employees looking for new jobs. Employee morale is at an all-time low, which might explain the failings in quality control. Due to the somewhat isolated location of the plant, re-placing these employees could be difficult. McRoberts is particularly afraid of los-ing David McNulty, who is an old-timer with a number of practical solutions and experience in both Engineering and Production. Dickerson is afraid of losing his best employee, Robert Smith, whom he brought over from the United States. Smith was recently criticized by Masters for initiating changes in their new model in an attempt to solve some of the problems in it. Smith had not cleared the changes with Masters, and although he had solved one of the basic problems with the model, all he got for his effort was criticism. Dickerson has been in-formed by Smith and other staff members that if he cannot "protect" them from Masters, they will consider quitting. Unfortunately, Masters considers the clearing of all decisions through him a must, which is typical of his "hub and spoke" con-cept of organizational structure (like a wheel, all communication must go through the center (the hub), making decision making centralized). This structure has, unfortunately, prevented interdepartmental cooperation, which has only made a bad situation worse. Masters's criticisms about cost efficiency and quality control has created pressure on both Engineering and Production. McRoberts and Dickerson have started blaming each other. Production has claimed that the specifications have been unclear, and Engineering has claimed that Production does not know how to read the drawings. Pressure has mounted to the point where both McRoberts and Dickerson have decided to call a meeting to air and, they hope, to solve the problems. McRoberts and Dickerson see three main prob-lems:

1. Problems created by Masters's management style, resulting in employee discontent.
2. Practical problems of the factory's outmoded production system.
3. Conflicts between the Engineering and Production Departments.

Both Dickerson and McRoberts know that they must confront Masters, and that they must work out a strategy for how to deal with him. Dickerson also knows that the costs of the conversion equal the sum of last year's profits, al-though this expense will be spread over a number of years. Thus, he knows he will meet resistance on this suggestion and has worked out estimates showing that an assembly-line will reduce production time per unit from ten to eight hours. This will result in savings that will pay for the £2 million in three years. Finally, Dickerson and McRoberts must work out their differences in front of Masters to show him that they are trying to solve problems. They hope that this will create some goodwill with Masters, prompting him to stay off their backs. Otherwise, growing tensions will result in insurmountable personnel problems. In preparing for the meeting with Masters, Dickerson and McRoberts will not only have to take into consideration Masters's personality, but also the following barri-ers to change:

1. **Value barriers.** The proposed changes conflict with certain individuals' perceptions (in this case, those of Masters) and philosophies of how the company should be run and how employees should be managed. In this latter

concern, Masters must be made aware of the importance of treating professionals as professionals.

2. **Power barriers.** Certain changes, especially reorganization, threaten certain individuals' positions and power in a company. In this case, Masters may perceive the meeting as a plot to undermine his power through greater employee freedom and decentralized decision making, which in turn would conflict with his perception of how a company should be run. He may fear that his "hub and spoke" approach may be undermined by interdepartmental cooperation. At the same time that he wants greater cost efficiency, he might be afraid of the interdepartmental cooperation that may be necessary to achieve it because he may lose control of the decision-making process.

3. **Psychological barriers.** These barriers often come from a general fear of change, resulting from personal insecurity and the resulting preference for maintaining the status quo. Does Masters's top-down approach stem from personal insecurity that will make him resistant to all change? If so, how can Dickerson and McRoberts approach him to overcome his fear?

POINTS FOR DISCUSSION

1. Discuss bosses you have had, and give concrete examples of what made them good or bad bosses.
2. What are common mistakes that bosses make, and how, in a diplomatic way, can they be made to see these mistakes?

CASE ACTIVITIES

Productive Criticism of Management Styles

Dickerson and McRoberts have called a meeting with the following people (who will be played by you, the students):

> Tom Masters, President
> James Dickerson, Production Manager
> David McNulty, Production Department Employee
> William McRoberts, Engineering Manager
> Robert Smith, Engineering Department Employee

The stated purpose of the meeting is to work out problems between Engineering and Production and to consider remodeling the factory's production facility. An unstated item on the agenda is Masters's management style. Masters suspects this and feels threatened. The first item (see the agenda in Figure 8-1) is basically designed to create goodwill with Masters, but concrete results must be achieved. Here you can draw from the experience of Smith and McNulty, who should contribute concrete suggestions on how to improve cooperation, such as including Production people in Engineering operations so that they can become

```
Jan. 17, 199_

12:00 P.M.

1. Cooperation between engineering and production
2. Assembly-line production and factory remodeling.
3. Any other business.
```

Figure 8-1   Agenda for Meeting

familiarized with the workings of Engineering and make suggestions, in terms of production problems, that might arise from certain design features. McNulty has worked in both Engineering and Production and would be the perfect partner to develop interdepartmental cooperation, as he understands both sides of the engineering/production process.

After reaching some concrete solutions, move on to item two on the agenda, where once again Engineering and Production exhibit a desire to cooperate to develop an assembly-line system. The second part of this item is to convince Masters to convert production to an assembly-line system. Masters is skeptical on three grounds: (1) cost; (2) the fact that the factory will have to be closed, and thus the problems of meeting delivery schedules and loss of sales and possible layoffs that such a closing will entail; and (3) a general skepticism about loss of control over the decision-making process (see the list of barriers to change on pages 71–72). The representatives from Engineering and Production will have to develop arguments and suggestions to convince Masters, such as employees working overtime to build up inventories to cover the period when the factory will be closed, cooperation between Engineering and Production in designing and building the assembly-line that will save money and keep the layoffs at a minimum, and so on. Smith has designed assembly-lines before and could provide the drawings.

The final item on the agenda, though not stated as such, will address Masters's management style, the problems it is causing, and the effects on the company and its personnel.

Sales	Net Profit after Taxes	Return on Sales	Market Share in Great Britain
£40,000,000	£2,000,000	5%	4.5%

Figure 8-2   Profit and Loss Figures for Sterling Forklift, Ltd. for 199—(the previous year). These figures reflect a low net profit of 5 percent, which suggests a need for increased efficiency.

In preparation for this meeting, all those students playing Masters, Dickerson, McRoberts, Smith, and McNulty will meet to develop their roles and contributions. Let us say there are four students playing Masters. They will meet to define their attitudes toward the first two items on the agenda and their fears and attitudes toward the final, unstated item on the agenda. Those playing Dickerson will meet to discuss what they can contribute to a cooperative effort between Production and Engineering, in order to build a case that will convince Masters of the necessity of converting the factory to an assembly-line system. Those playing McRoberts will discuss what they can contribute to create better cooperation between Engineering and Production. Those playing Smith and those playing McNulty will discuss their roles and contributions to the meeting. Finally, students playing the four employees will also discuss how to confront Masters about his management style. After each participant has prepared his or her role, the Dickersons, McRobertses, McNulties and Smiths, who will be performing together in the meeting, will get together and discuss a common strategy. Those playing Masters will continue their discussion of their role. Thus, the two preparation phases will look like this (based on a class of 20 students):

Phase 1

Group 1	Group 2	Group 3	Group 4	Group 5
4 Masters	4 McRoberts	4 Dickersons	4 McNulties	4 Smiths

Phase 2

Group 1	Group 2	Groups 3, 4, and 5
4 Masters	1 McRoberts	Same composition as Group 2
	1 Dickerson	
	1 McNulty	
	1 Smith	

The Meeting

You will hold as many meetings as you have persons playing each character, with one Masters, Dickerson, McRoberts, Smith, and McNulty in each meeting. After each meeting is concluded, have a discussion in which all the groups discuss how they dealt with Masters and what conclusions were reached. The participants should make the following contributions:

McRoberts:

Should chair the meeting and make a brief statement about how he and Dickerson have established a team consisting of employees from both Engineering and Production to work to create better communication between the two departments.

Smith and McNulty:

Should provide details about how this team approach works in practice, including how employees develop drawings for products in order to avoid misunderstanding and to take into account ease of production when products are being designed. Smith and McNulty should also contribute to the second item on the agenda, the assembly-line, with drawings of an assembly-line and an explanation of how it will be more efficient.

Dickerson:

Should introduce item two on the agenda and then turn the discussion over to McNulty and Smith, who will give details and present an argument in favor of the assembly-line approach. Dickerson will also diplomatically introduce the question of Masters's leadership style and make an appeal for greater decentralization of decision making and less pressure on employees, based on a concern for the employees and the overall success of the company.

Masters:

Will act his role according to the personality described in the case.

LANGUAGE MASTERY EXERCISE

Diplomatic Language

Dealing with personal conflicts such as the ones in this case requires the use of diplomatic language. In the writing section on "Word Choice and Attitudes" in Case 7 (page 65), a series of diplomatic formulations is outlined. Working in pairs and using those formulations, the hints given below, or formulations which you choose yourself, revise the following sentences. Remember that you want to appeal to Masters's desire for cost efficiency and quality control, while not threatening him.

1. We want to install an assembly-line production system.

    Hint: We feel that . . .
    Competing factories with assembly-lines . . .

2. The present system of production is not efficient.

    Hint: If we installed assembly-line production, we could . . .

3. Your attitude toward us is destructive.

    Hint: We feel that we would perform better if . . .

4. Your leadership style prevents necessary cooperation between Engineering and Production.

    Hint: Cooperation would be easier if . . .

5. You are pressuring us too much.

    Hint: Pressuring us slightly less would . . .

6. We must have the opportunity to cooperate.

    Hint: Wouldn't it be better if . . .

7. It is obviously cheaper and more efficient to have assembly-line production.

   Hint: What would you say if we could show you that . . .

8. Our best people are going to quit if changes are not made around here.

   Hint: We are afraid that . . .

9. Why are you so stubborn and why can't you listen to us?

   Hint: Sometimes we feel . . .

10. We demand more decentralized authority.

   Hint: We would like to propose . . .

WRITING: MEMOS

Masters should write a memo to the employees expressing his perception of the outcome of the meeting and proposing any planned changes in his managerial approach.

Dickerson and McNulty should write a memo to the Production staff stating how the decisions at the meeting will affect production routines, including cooperation with Engineering if any agreement on this item was reached.

McRoberts and Smith should write a memo similar to that written by Dickerson and McNulty, only directed to the Engineering staff.

VOCABULARY

accountability, *n.*   Responsibility for the outcome. The person who is *accountable* enjoys the responsibility of making his or her own decisions, but is also responsible for the success or failure of the operation.

to air a problem, *v.*   To openly discuss a problem in hopes of solving it.

authoritarian, *adj.*   A personal or leadership style in which all power and decision making are vested in the leader or boss.

bottom-up, *adj.*   A managerial style in which employees have an influence on decision making. (See *top-down*).

to breathe down someone's neck, *v.*   To constantly put pressure on someone and check repeatedly on what they are doing.

to call on the carpet, *v.*   To criticize someone for bad on-the-job performance.

to collaborate, *v.*   To work together with others.

collaboration, *n.*   Working together, often on a specific project.

company culture, *n.*   The shared values, beliefs, and ways of doing things in a company.

compromise, *n.*   Settling differences by mutual concession.

to compromise, *v.*   To settle differences by mutual concession.

conflict, *n.*   The blocking of goals and expectations of one individual or group by another individual or group, usually leading to frustration.

conflict resolution, *n.*   The solving of conflicts. (See Business Organization and Management textbooks for conflict resolution strategies.)

to confront, *v.*   To face someone and express disagreement.

confrontation, *n.*   An open dispute.

to cooperate *v.*   To work together.

cooperation, *n.*   Working together. *interdepartmental cooperation* refers to cooperation between departments like Production and Engineering.

decentralized management, *n.*   A management style in which decision making is delegated to employees at lower levels in the organization.

decision-making process, *n.*   The process by which decisions are made, which also involves deciding who is to make the decisions.

to delegate, *v.*   To assign power and/or responsibilities.

delegation, *n.*   The act of giving the power of decision making to employees at levels below that of the one in charge.

eye for figures, *adj.*   To be good at, and interested in, anything dealing with numbers — in this case, accounting and profit and loss.

to get wind of something, *v.*   To hear about something indirectly.

hardheaded, *adj.*   Stubborn.

horizontal communication, *n.*   Communication between departments at the same level in the organization (for example, between Engineering and Production).

incremental cash flow, *n.*   The amount of additional cash receipts expected for a period of a time if a project is undertaken.

to iron out/work out the bugs, *v.*   To improve a product so as to solve technical problems.

job satisfaction, *n.*   Satisfaction stemming from working conditions and the atmosphere in an organization.

managerial style, *n.*   See your Business Organization and Management textbook for a description of various managerial styles and their consequences.

MBO, *n.*   Management by Objective.

open channels, *n.*   A condition in which (a) employees are free to communicate their ideas to management, and (b) management takes these ideas seriously. In an open-channels system there is **vertical communication**.

payback period, *n.*   The time it will take to earn back the total amount of money invested in a project.

personality conflict, *n.*   A situation in which two or more people do not get along due to differences in personality.

stickler, *n.*   One who insists on something; a *stickler for costs* would be someone who insisted on keeping costs low.

top-down, *n.*   A management style in which all decisions are made at the top.

BANKING

Smith Brothers and Florida Central

CULTURAL BACKGROUND: LOAN APPLICATIONS

Capital for small businesses is usually provided by banks. In the United States, when a bank loan officer interviews a small business owner who is applying for a loan, he or she may try to evaluate the personal characteristics of the loan applicant as well as get answers to financial questions. The personal aspect of the interview is to determine how serious the loan applicant is, as well as his or her qualities as a businessperson because the loan officer naturally wants to make sure the bank gets its money back. One aspect of the loan application process in the United States that may vary from many other cultures is the importance of the personal contact between the loan officer and applicant, and the loan officer's resulting evaluation of the applicant.

CASE

Smith Brothers Building Materials Company, Inc. was founded by Wilbur Smith in 1942. Elmer and Zachary Smith, the two youngest sons of the founder, have been managing the company since 1985. All of the company stock is held by a family trust. The company operates six stores throughout the state of Florida. Two stores are located in Orlando, one in Miami, one in West Palm Beach, one in Sarasota, and one in St. Petersburg. Smith Brothers employs a total of 195 people.

Throughout the years, Smith Brothers has utilized the banking services provided by the First Federal Bank of Orlando. Unfortunately, however, Zachary Smith has become dissatisfied with his relationship with First Federal for a variety of reasons, including the high turnover among account officers. Zachary believes that the level and quality of service received from First Federal has declined because of this personnel problem. Florida Central, First Federal's biggest competitor, has tried unsuccessfully for years to solicit business, trust, and personal associations from the family and its business. In light of the current situation, Zachary Smith has been seriously considering developing a relationship with Florida Central. The company's long history of profitable operations and the excellent reputation of the current management make Smith Brothers a very attractive customer for any bank. Although Zachary may be persuaded to develop a relationship with Florida Central, he intends to maintain relationships with a number of different banks to insure that he always receives the level and quality of service that he desires.

A Smith Brothers loan application at Florida Central Bank, dated March 12, 1995, requests a $2.5 million line of credit with the following terms: an interest rate of the national prime rate plus .3 percent, unrestricted use of funds, and no personal guaranty (i.e., the Smith Brothers will not be personally responsible for repayment of the loan if the company is unable to pay it back). Zachary and Elmer Smith have enclosed a statement expressing the reasons for their request. In this document, they assert that the loan is needed to meet seasonal working capital needs related to the building materials industry. The brothers also indicate that they will increase the amount of their loan payments during their slow season, when they would have less money tied up in inventory. Financial statements prepared from the records of the company are also included in the application for examination by the loan officers.

Although Smith Brothers Building Materials appears to be an excellent company, the loan officers at Florida Central have requested that Zachary and Elmer Smith meet with them to discuss the particulars of the loan application. The two Florida Central loan officers, Alexandra Hamilton and Joshua Hall, have some reservations about the loan; they would like to gather more information about the current financial position of the organization and the company's reasons for switching banks before making any decisions about whether or not to grant the brothers' request for a loan. The loan officers must make a determination about the character of the borrowers, their creditworthiness, their capacity to repay the loan, and their ability to put up collateral to secure it. After reviewing the application together, Hamilton and Hall have prepared a number of questions for their interview with the Smith brothers. While the bank has been courting this family's business for many years, the loan officers must negotiate a deal that provides the best possible return for the bank. The loan officers must balance the benefits of securing the Smith family's business against the potential profits for the bank.

Hamilton and Hall have compiled the following list of questions and requests for the Smith brothers. They believe that this line of questioning, along with the additional data requested, will provide them with enough information to make a good decision concerning the creditworthiness of Smith Brothers Building Materials. Students playing the roles of the Smith brothers should prepare answers to these questions, which are based on Hamilton and Hall's analysis of the Smith Brothers' accounts. These students must study the accounts and prepare an explanation in response to these questions. Remember that Hall and Hamilton will also be evaluating the Smith brothers' character and business sense. Thus, those who play the roles of Zachary and Elmer Smith must appear serious and be able to answer these questions in a convincing manner.

1. Would it be possible for you to provide us with audited financial statements? In addition, we would like more detailed information about the subsidiaries.

2. Why have accounts receivable more than doubled in the past year? Have your internal controls changed? We would also like to examine a current accounts-receivable aging schedule if possible.

3. Why were assets shifted from cash to marketable equity securities in 1994? Has your cash management strategy changed?

4. Could you give us an idea of what you intend to do with the loan proceeds?

5. Why did inventory show a drastic increase in 1994?

6. Finally, we would like to discuss the loan terms that you requested in your application. First, failure to obtain a personal guarantee for a loan violates bank policy concerning the extension of credit. Second, the interest rate you requested of prime rate plus .3 percent would prevent the bank from recognizing any type of profit. This rate is far too low to be attractive to the bank. Also, would you object to providing some piece of property as collateral if the loan committee deems it necessary?

The Smith brothers have been informed of the issues to be addressed in their interview with the loan officers by a friend employed at the bank. This has enabled them to effectively prepare for their meeting with Hamilton and Hall.

POINTS FOR DISCUSSION

1. Discuss what criteria a loan officer would use in evaluating an application such as the one in this case. Consult a banker to get his or her criteria.

2. As a loan officer, what might make you skeptical about granting this loan?

3. What questions might a loan officer ask in the interview with Zachary and Elmer Smith to determine the soundness of the business?

4. How reasonable are the terms requested by Smith Brothers?

CASE ACTIVITIES

Applying for a Loan

Half of the groups will prepare the roles of the Smith brothers and develop convincing arguments to support their loan application, preparing answers to the questions above, as well as working out a position in terms of the interest rate negotiations. The other half of the groups will prepare the roles of the loan officers by analyzing the balance sheet from Smith Brothers and reviewing the questions to be asked of Zachary and Elmer Smith. Try to understand the questions in light of the balance sheet (see Figure 9-1). For the meeting of the Smiths and the loan officers, the class will be divided into groups of four (the two Smiths and the two loan officers). There will be as many meetings as there are teams of Smiths and loan officers. In the meeting, the loan officers will ask the questions above and will negotiate the interest rate of the loan and any other conditions they feel are necessary. At the same time, the loan officers will formulate an opinion as to whether or not the loan should be granted, based on the conditions established, the creditworthiness of Smith Brothers, and the character of the two brothers.

SMITH BROTHERS BUILDING MATERIALS
Balance Sheet
December 31, 1994

Assets	12/31/93	12/31/94
Current Assets		
Cash	$1,542,000	$323,000
Marketable Securities	287,000	1,281,753
Accounts Receivable — Gross	368,000	991,491
Reserve for Bad Debt	−42,000	−84,000
Accounts Receivable — Net	326,000	907,491
Inventory	3,985,000	4,516,000
Total Current Assets	**6,140,000**	**7,028,244**
Noncurrent Assets		
Prepaids	52,000	78,000
Due from Officers	85,000	85,000
Due from Subsidiaries	1,315,000	1,523,000
Total Fixed Assets	1,217,000	978,000
Accumulated Depreciation	−608,500	−487,000
Net Fixed Assets	608,500	491,000
Total Noncurrent Assets	**2,060,500**	**2,177,000**
Total Assets	**8,200,500**	**$9,205,244**
Liabilities		
Current Liabilities		
Accounts Payable	$1,349,000	$1,457,000
Accruals	394,000	372,000
Taxes Payable	160,000	142,000
Total Current Liabilities	**1,903,000**	**1,971,000**

continued

Figure 9-1   Balance sheet

continued		
Noncurrent Liabilities		
Deferred Taxes	17,500	29,000
Total Liabilities	**1,920,500**	**2,000,000**
Equity		
Common	650,000	650,000
Additional — PIC	20,000	20,000
Retained Earnings	5,610,000	6,535,244
Total Equity	**6,280,000**	**7,205,244**
Total Equity and Liabilities	**8,200,500**	**9,205,244**

Figure 9-1   Balance sheet *(continued)*

The Meeting

Hold the meeting between the loan officers and the Smith brothers. After all the groups have completed their meetings, hold a class discussion in which you address the results of the various meetings. What did the loan officers decide about granting the loan and on what terms? What were the main factors that led to their decision?

LANGUAGE MASTERY EXERCISE

Informal Meetings

This is a more informal meeting than in Case 3 ("Other People's Money"), and the vocabulary used reflects the situation. Learn these phrases for use in the meeting. Test your mastery of them by working in pairs and asking each other for sentences for opening, asking someone else's opinion, agreeing, and so on.

OPENING

JOSHUA HALL (JH):   Thank you for coming. We would like to take a closer look at your application and ask some questions.

QUESTIONS AND ANSWERS

JH: Perhaps we should first look at your sales figures for 199 ___ .
They seem flat. Could you explain that?

ZACHARY SMITH (ZS): Yes, I think that I can explain that.
A simple explanation is . . .

JH: Second, why were assets shifted from cash to marketable equity in 199 ___ ? Has your cash management strategy changed?

ZS: Yes, with falling interest rates and a rise in the stock market, we felt that it was more advantageous to have some of our assets in securities.

SOLICITING SOMEONE ELSE'S COMMENTS OR OPINION

JH: Alexandra, do you have any questions?
JH: Alexandra, what's your opinion?

CONCLUDING A SUBJECT

ALEXANDRA HAMILTON (AH): Mr. Smith, do you have anything else you want to add?

INTERRUPTING

AH: Excuse me, Mr. Smith, but I have a question.

MOVING ON

JH: Could we go on to question four?

CREATING A POSITIVE CLIMATE

ZS: I think you will agree that . . .

STATING PREFERENCES

ZS: We'd rather . . .
We'd prefer to . . .

PRESENTING THE OTHER SIDE

ZS: On the other hand, . . .
We must not forget . . .
However, we must take into consideration . . .

AGREEING

JH: I agree with you [*neutral*].
I completely/totally agree with you [*strong*].

ZS: I disagree [*neutral*].
I completely/totally disagree [*strong*].

AH: I'm afraid that I can't quite agree [*more diplomatic*].
Have you considered the consequences of your position [*to raise questions and get the other side to reconsider its position*]?

ZS: I can see your point, but . . . [*creates a common understanding while also presenting disagreement*].

EXPRESSING RESERVATIONS

JH: I cannot completely agree with your position.
I have some reservations about your proposal.

WRITING: LOAN APPLICATION RESPONSE LETTER

Write a letter from the loan officer either approving or rejecting Smith Brothers' loan application. If you have decided to grant the loan, state its conditions (i.e., interest rate, the necessity to provide a guaranty, and so on). If you refuse the loan, do so in a polite manner.

VOCABULARY

accounts-payable aging, *n.* A schedule that lists and analyzes the accounts payable in terms of the length of time outstanding.

accounts-receivable aging, *n.* A schedule that lists and analyzes the receivable accounts in terms of the length of their time past due.

acid test ratio, *n.* A measure of liquidity; the ratio is determined by dividing current assets, less inventories, by current liabilities.

capacity, *n.* The ability to repay the loan, usually determined by examining current and future financial positions.

character, *n.* Features or attributes that make up and distinguish the individual; when extending credit, an understanding of the applicant's character makes it possible to evaluate the risk involved in granting them a loan.

collateral, *n.* Property, such as securities, inventories, land, equipment, or accounts receivable, that is pledged by a borrower to protect the interests of the lender; the borrower would have to forfeit this asset if they became unable to make the required payments.

compensating balance, *n.* The average demand (checking account) a bank requires a regular borrower to maintain as part of the loan agreement. It is often 10–20 percent of the face amount of the loan.

credit, *n.* An amount or sum placed at a person's disposal by a bank.

current ratio, *n.* The ratio of current assets to current liabilities; a measure of an organization's liquidity.

inventory turnover, *n.*   A measure of how quickly the inventory is sold; computed by dividing the cost of goods sold by the average inventory.

line of credit, *n.*   A formal or informal understanding between a bank and a borrower that indicates how much credit the bank will extend to the borrower.

liquidity, *n.*   The ability to meet obligations as they become due. A firm that is liquid can, by definition, support its operational goals.

marketable equities, *n.*   Stocks, bonds, and other investments that are easily and quickly sold to obtain cash.

operating profit, *n.*   Gross profit less operating expenses.

promissory note, *n.*   A written document signed when a bank loan is approved. The note specifies the amount borrowed, the interest rate, the repayment schedule, any collateral put up as security for the loan, and any other terms and conditions to which the bank and borrower may have agreed.

receivables, *n.*   Money owed to a company due to goods or services delivered, but not yet paid for.

INTRODUCTION TO OPEN-ENDED CASES

The remaining cases in this book are open-ended. This means that not all the information necessary to solve them is provided in the cases. Each group will have to research the topic and provide the material to solve the cases. The intention is to help develop information-finding skills to go along with the skills that have already been developed in the previous cases. Another feature of these cases is that they are closely related to local business conditions or are classic cases in the industry (such as Case 14, "Saturn: Can American Automobile Manufacturers Compete with the Japanese?"). Thus, they provide the opportunity to become familiar with actual business questions and problems. Once again, everyone will be expected to play an active role in solving the cases, and will have to seek out information.

Before solving the cases, the class should brainstorm (suggest ideas with no limits) as to where you can best find the necessary information to solve the cases. This activity is invaluable because it will help develop creative thinking, which is one of the most important skills in dealing successfully with the current business climate in an age of information technology. Even though gathering information may be an unfamiliar task, brainstorming will help you develop creative means of obtaining necessary information, a skill that will be very useful in the future.

MARKETING

Penetrating the Market with Long-range Golf Clubs and Bags

CULTURAL BACKGROUND: INFORMATION GATHERING

Marketing techniques vary from country to country. If this case is set in a non-English-speaking country, use that country's approach. If the case is set in an English-speaking country, contact marketing students to get their input on how they would solve the case, and/or read marketing textbooks to get relevant information. Remember, the cases in this book are designed to encourage the development of information-gathering skills, so use the sources of information available to you. The case provides you with the basic information, but discussions with others can provide even more information that will be useful in solving the case.

CASE

The purpose of this case is to develop a marketing strategy for Long-range products. The case will be based on conditions in the country where you are presently residing. Thus, you will have to do the necessary market analysis based on information to which you should have access. This case is realistic, in that you would have to do the same market analysis if you were going to introduce a new product. *Do not assume that the conclusions regarding your contract in "Long-range Golf Equipment Seeks a Distributor" (Case 4) are necessarily valid in this case. Your means of distribution will depend on other factors, such as your market analysis, segmentation, and market mix (the four P's: product, price, place, and promotion). Remember that all these factors are interdependent; thus, you cannot choose a means of distribution independent of the market analysis, segmentation, and the four P's.*

POINTS FOR DISCUSSION

1. What are the four P's in marketing and what do decisions involving them consist of? Expand on the information provided in this case by either reading marketing textbooks or interviewing marketing students or experts.
2. What are the basic aspects of market research?

CASE ACTIVITIES

Developing a Marketing Strategy

Each group will develop a marketing strategy that will include the following information:

1. Market analysis
2. Market segmentation and selection of target group(s)
3. Positioning
4. The four P's (product, price, place, and promotion)

Market Analysis

How much is currently being spent on golf clubs and bags in your target market? What percentage of that amount is being spent on clubs and bags in the price range of the equipment you produce? What is the predicted growth in sales in this market over the next five years? Answers to these questions will help you determine what clubs you will launch in the market. We assume that you produce a full range of golf clubs, and that only some of the lines will be appropriate for your target market (it is up to you to determine what range of golf clubs Long-range produces). Use established market forecasting tools to determine these figures, or obtain accurate figures from the national golf association in your country. Analyze the market in terms of (1) demographics — age, gender, and geographic concentration; (2) economics — salaries and professions; and (3) cultural factors — lifestyles, self-image, aspirations. Who are your major competitors and, realistically speaking, what percentage of the market share can you expect to capture in three years?

Market Segmentation and Selection of Target Group(s)

Segmentation involves dividing the market into segments according to criteria such as age, gender, income, occupation, class, location, lifestyle, self-perception (the person's image of himself or herself), and usage level (the Sunday golfer versus the impassioned golfer who plays as often as possible). Once you have segmented the market, you must choose the target market for your market penetration. Choosing a target market involves finding the segment of the total market that you will strive to capture. This will form the basis for your positioning and market mix (the four P's).

Positioning

In positioning you will try to choose the right product(s) and give them the right image to capture the chosen target market. For example, you may choose to emphasize the high-tech clubs in your range if your target market is avid golfers who view themselves as good golfers who could be even better with the right clubs. Or you might try to appeal to the Sunday golfer who needs a forgiving club (a club that produces a good shot even if the ball is not perfectly hit). In addition, you will consider product decisions. How do prospective customers decide what to buy — are they buying based on needs, wants, or perceived benefits? What criteria (such as quality, price, and so on) are used to evaluate the product? What information (such as data on score improvement, style and status, the pros who use the clubs, and so on) is necessary to convince customers to buy?

Based on your target market, what range of clubs (how many different lines), and what end of the market (up-market, popular, or someplace in between) do you wish to promote in the beginning? What about golf accessories like bags, shoes, gloves, and the like? How much do you intend to launch in the beginning; and if you intend to increase your line, how quickly do you want to do so?

The Four P's: Product, Price, Place, and Promotion

The four P's must be in accordance with what you have outlined above. Marketing must be an extremely integrated process, because each individual element influences and is influenced by the other elements.

PRODUCT: Which of the products that you currently produce are you going to choose for your market penetration? Naturally, this will depend on your target group. If you are targeting the discerning golfer, you will choose the upper-market range of your line. This decision also involves the choice of products other than golf clubs. Are you going to concentrate on golf clubs alone, or are you also going to launch accessories (bags, clothes, and so on) as well? Are you going to launch everything all at once or phase different products in over time?

PRICE: Your choice of target market and products will, of course, influence the price range of the equipment you plan to launch.

PLACE (CHANNEL OF DISTRIBUTION): The two P's above will influence your choice of distribution network. If you are targeting the discerning golfer and positioning up-market clubs to capture this market, you will want to distribute them through pro shops (shops at golf courses run by a professional golfer) or other exclusive shops. On the other hand, the Sunday golfer who decides on the basis of price rather than quality may be best reached through department stores like Sears in the United States or Alders in England.

PROMOTION: First, you will have to determine your promotional goals. Then you will have to establish a promotion budget that will in turn affect your decisions about promotional mix. You should break down the total amount you intend to spend the first year for each item in your promotional mix, including:

1. *Public relations*. For example, you might hire a golf pro to do a series of golf clinics using Long-range clubs.
2. *Advertising*. Break down your advertising budget into (a) television, (b) radio, (c) newspapers, and (d) magazines.
3. *Sales promotion*. For example, you might hold contests for top salespersons and for buyers of Long-range clubs and bags.

4. *Personal selling.* This item would include commissions, salaries, and operating expenses for your distributor or sales force.

Once you have decided on your mix, you must decide how to effectively use each of the four P's. What is your public relations and sales promotion strategy? What media channels and approach are you going to use? In developing this strategy, you have to work closely with the market segmentation and target market people in your group. The characteristics (life-style, self-perception, attitudes, class, occupation, and so on) of your target market are important factors in designing an advertising strategy. After gaining a thorough knowledge of your target group(s), sketch out the type of television and radio spots you want to use (describe a typical spot in terms of what will be said and done), and lay out advertisements for newspapers and magazines. Explain how these spots and advertisements will convey the intended image of your product and convince the potential buyer (that is, describe the strategy behind your campaign). Based on your budget, provide information about frequency and channels (which television and radio stations and which newspapers and magazines) to be used.

After discussing these market strategy areas in your group, assign the tasks of presentation to each of your group members. One member should handle the market analysis and provide answers to the following questions:

1. How much is currently being spent in the golf club and bag sector?
2. What percentage is being spent on clubs and bags in the price range of the equipment you plan to launch?
3. What is the predicted growth in sales in golf clubs and bags in your market over the next five years?
4. Who are your major competitors, and what market share can you expect to capture in three years?

Use overheads and/or other graphic representations to present your findings.

One member should handle segmentation and selection of the target market. Use charts to depict and present your target group(s). State clearly the characteristics of your target market, such as (a) age, (b) gender, (c) occupation, (d) income, (e) class, (f) life-style and self-perception, and (g) user frequency. Explain why, given these characteristics, you have chosen this segment.

One to two members should present the four P's, working in close conjunction with the market segmentation/target market people in your group. These members should show how your four P's coincide with, and are geared toward, the target market.

In presenting your promotional campaign, make graphics or layouts of your intended ads, and explain them in terms of their impact on the target market you want to reach. For the television and radio spots, either tape existing spots and explain how similar spots could be used to sell *your* clubs and bags, or sketch a scenario orally, covering a thirty-second spot (that is, describe what television viewers or radio listeners will see or hear in your ads.). Discuss frequency and timing of your spots or advertisements, as well as channels (which television and radio stations and which newspapers and magazines). Present an overhead with your promotional budget. Discuss public relations and sales promotion ideas. Be creative!

One group member should present your channel(s) of distribution. Will you primarily use pro shops, general sporting goods shops or department stores, or a mix? What channels would best reach your target market and represent the image of your product that you are trying to promote?

The emphasis in this presentation should be on being professional and creative. To achieve this, do your homework so that you know what you are talking about and are prepared. Do a trial run so that your presentations flow smoothly and are tied together. Use your imagination and consult other sources of information, such as your national golf association and distributors of golf equipment.

LANGUAGE MASTERY EXERCISE

Professional Presentation

This case requires a group presentation, so here are some examples of the vocabulary needed to make a professional presentation.

GREETING

Good morning / afternoon / evening.

INTRODUCTION (OF THE GROUP AND THE TOPIC)

Note: Each group should choose an anchorperson who introduces the group and subject and provides a conclusion. This person can also make part of the presentation, depending on the number of members in the group.

We represent Marketing Research, Inc. and are going to present our recommendations for the launching of Long-range Golf Equipment.

Our group consists of Eva, who will present the segmentation of the market and target market selection; Thomas, who will discuss positioning; Roberta, who will cover product and price; and myself, Alice. I will discuss place and promotion.

As I have outlined, our presentation will analyze the market potential for Long-range clubs and bags including segmentation, target market, positioning, and the four P's. First, Eva will present the segmentation of the market and target market selection. Eva. (Eva should then step forward, say "Thank you, Alice," and begin her presentation.)

OPENING STATEMENTS

Let me begin by saying . . .
I would like to begin by . . .

CHANGING THE SUBJECT

Now that we have looked at the segmentation, let us look at the selection of the target market.

Note: To make smooth transitions, use sequencing words such as *first, second, third*, or *first, next, then*. In addition, use transition expressions such as the following:

For addition

In addition
Equally important
Furthermore

For comparison

Similarly
Likewise

For contrast

On the other hand
However
Despite
Although

To show cause and effect

Thus
Therefore
Consequently
As a result

HIGHLIGHTS

Most important, . . .
What you must remember, . . .
Interestingly enough, . . .

CONCLUSION

In conclusion, . . .
In summary, . . .

Practice structuring your presentation in advance of the in-class performance, using the above structuring devices.

WRITING: MARKET REPORT

Write a report to the management of Long-range Sports Equipment in which you summarize your (1) market analysis, (2) market segmentation and the target market you have chosen, as well as why you chose this segment, (3) a strategy for positioning Long-range products, and (4) the four P's.

VOCABULARY

advertising, *n.*   The promotion of an idea, goods, or services through the media.

advertising agency, *n.*   An agency whose function it is to develop an advertising campaign.

brand, *n.*   A name associated with a specific product (for example, *Coca-Cola, Ford, General Electric*). A *trademark* is a brand that has been given legal protection.

break-even analysis, *n.*   A technique to discover what volume of sales is necessary to reach a break-even point (where the seller covers his or her costs).

cannibalization, *n.*   A situation in which one product reaches a market share at the expense of other products in the same market produced by the same producer.

disposable income, *n.*   The personal income left after deductions for social security, insurance, and taxes.

F.O.B. (free on board), *n.*   Any point to which the transportation costs are born by the seller and at which the title passes to the buyer.

implementation, *n.*   The putting into practice of a marketing strategy.

margin, *n.*   The difference between the cost of production of an item and its selling price.

market penetration, *n.*   Entering a new market with a product.

market share, *n.*   The percentage of a total market that a product has.

marketing mix, *n.*   The combination of factors to be considered in marketing: price, promotion (advertising and personal sales), place (channels of distribution), and product. This is traditionally known as the four P's.

marketing research, *n.*   Research done to determine the conditions and potentials of a market.

positioning, *n.*   Meeting the needs of a market by either developing a new product, altering an existing product, or changing the image of an existing product through advertising.

pricing, *n.*   Setting a price on a product or service.

prime time, *n.*   The viewing time on television when most people are watching (usually considered to be between 7 and 11 P.M.).

product differentiation, *n.* Any difference (real or imaginary) intended to set a product apart from its competitors and, it is hoped, make it more attractive to the consumer.

pro shops, *n.* Golf equipment shops run by a professional golfer (the *pro*). The pro may give advice on selecting the proper equipment and give golf lessons. These shops tend to be up-market.

segmentation, *n.* The dividing of a market into segments on the basis of geographical areas, demographics (income, age, gender, ethnic groups, and the like), lifestyles, and attitudes.

target market, *n.* After segmentation, the segment of the market at which a company chooses to aim their product.

telemarketing, *n.* Using the telephone to sell a product.

MARKETING

Costa de los Años de Oro

CULTURAL BACKGROUND: INFORMATION GATHERING

Please refer to the section on "Cultural Background: Information Gathering" in Case 10 (page 89) in preparation for this case.

CASE

On a recent vacation, you overheard a conversation between two older people (for the purposes of this case, if you live in Europe or Africa, your vacation was in the Canary Islands; if you live in Latin America, it was in the Caribbean; if you live in the Far East, it was in Bali, in which case you will have to change the name of the resort). The people you overheard were complaining about their vacations, and you found their complaints interesting. First, they complained about the lack of availability of extended-stay vacations — say six weeks to three months — for people in their age group. Second, they complained about being jammed in with the disco crowd, and the resulting noise, and so on. Third, they complained about the lack of activities for senior citizens. A couple of days later, you met a local contractor who had access to plots of land to build a resort. You asked for his business card and mentioned that you might be interested in a business deal.

POINTS FOR DISCUSSION

1. How important are people over 65 as a market, and what products could be successfully promoted in this market? (Try to think of products that are not currently being promoted in this market.)
2. Why is this an increasingly important market, or why is it not?
3. How important are travel and recreation for older people in your culture? Are these people's ideas about travel changing?

CASE ACTIVITIES

Market Research: Vacations for Senior Citizens

Upon returning to your country, you start investigating the possibility of a vacation community for senior citizens. You begin by carrying out the following market research to determine (a) if in fact there is a market for a senior citizens' resort and (b) what facilities and activities such a resort should contain. At the same time, you investigate the possibility of opening a travel bureau exclusively for senior citizens to serve that market.

Your market research should include the following:

Market Segmentation

Do a demographic study of the people in your market area to find out the numbers of senior citizens. Include a gender, income, and occupational status breakdown. (Also find out what percentage of this group is still working full- or part-time, and what percentage is available for long-term vacations.) Is there an imbalance between men and women? Obtain some general information about lifestyle and self-perception (the image they have of themselves, including user frequency, or the frequency of travel; vacation destination; average length of stay; and future travel plans). Also consider benefit segmentation (what people in this market area expect to get in exchange for the money invested, such as companionship, knowledge, excitement, and so on).

Target Market

Do a profile of your target group, including gender breakdown by percentage, marital status (are there a large number of singles?), preference in terms of the class of hotel facilities (rating from tourist to luxury or using the star system used by tour operators), and expectations in terms of what is offered by a resort. Investigate whether this market is being adequately served. If you find that it is not, move to the next step.

Positioning

Develop a concept to meet the needs of the market. Begin with your philosophy. What is your concept of vacationing and your attitude toward your target market? How do you view the needs, both personal and recreational, of this group? Include a design of the facilities you intend to build, showing how they will meet the needs of the target market. This design should be graphically represented by pictures of the total facility, with reference to specific facilities and services that your market survey has indicated that senior citizens want. It should also include room plans for rooms that are geared to the needs of people in this group. You should also provide activity schedules based on your market research.

In carrying out this survey, do both primary (if possible) and secondary research. The primary research can be done in the form of a questionnaire to be filled out by senior citizens, while the secondary research can be done through professional journals and by contacting travel agents or tour operators.

Considering your chosen positioning, briefly draw implications for the three remaining P's (you have already adequately described the product above): *price* and comfort level, *packages* in terms of length of stay and what the price includes, and *promotion* (what media will you use to promote the product?).

Here are a few tips for gathering the information necessary for this case.

Tour operators and travel bureaus should have a good deal of information about the market and brochures that you can use for your graphics. In addition, senior citizens' organizations might have some information. You might want to go to a social meeting of a group of senior citizens to have them fill out a market survey questionnaire. Don't forget your grandparents or parents. They may possess a wealth of information if they belong to your target market.

The presentation will consist of your group's presentation of the findings of your market survey, grouped in the categories outlined above: (1) segmentation, (2) target market, and (3) positioning (including a graphic presentation of the resort you are planning to develop to meet the demands of the market). You should assign each segment of the presentation to one or two group members so that every group member participates. Assign a group member the role of anchorperson; this person will give a general introduction and conclusion. Although all groups should come prepared to present, the teacher may choose two groups to present so that the presentation phase will not be too repetitious.

LANGUAGE MASTERY EXERCISES

Presentation

Refer to the "Professional Presentation" section of Case 10, "Penetrating the Market with Long-range Golf Clubs and Bags" (pages 93 – 94) for language suggestions.

Social Dialogues

Much business takes place in a social setting. Study the social English presented below and practice the dialogues in pairs until you feel comfortable with them. (The responses should come naturally without your having to think about them.)

INTRODUCTIONS

DAVID SANCHEZ (DS): Good morning, my name is David Sanchez [or, I am David Sanchez], and I represent the resort Costa de los Años de Oro.

ROBERTA JOHNSON (RJ): How do you do. Roberta Johnson, Tour Product Development Manager for Mansfield Tours. Pleased to meet you.

DS: Nice to meet you, Roberta/Ms. Johnson.

Note: Different cultures have different degrees of formality. In some cultures it is acceptable to start using first names from the beginning. However, if in doubt, use titles and last names.

INTRODUCTION OF OTHERS

DS: Ms. Johnson, I would like to introduce you to our Marketing Manager, Alberto Gomez (AG). Alberto, this is Roberta Johnson.

RJ: Pleased to meet you, Mr. Gomez.

AG: Nice meeting you, Ms. Johnson.

> *Note:* Mr. Gomez could also say simply, "Nice meeting you."

SEEING PEOPLE AGAIN

DS: Nice to see you again, Ms. Johnson. How have you been?

RJ: Fine, and you? How has business been?

> *Note:* Do not say, "Nice to *meet* you again." The verb *to meet* is only used for the first meeting.

INVITING AND ACCEPTING

RJ: Can I take you out to lunch?

DG: Thank you very much.

RJ: My pleasure. We can look at the contract over lunch.

DG: Sounds like a good idea.

REJECTING AN INVITATION

DAVID SMITH (DS): Bill, would you like to come over for dinner on Friday?

BILL JONES (BJ): I'd love to, but I'm afraid I am busy/have a commitment/will be out of town.

THANKING

DS: Thanks for helping me out with that contract. I never would have finished it without your help.

BJ: Think nothing of it. I was glad I could help you.
or You're quite welcome.
or Don't mention it.

WRITING: MARKETING REPORT

Write a report in which you summarize (1) your market segmentation and the target market you have chosen, as well as your reasons for choosing this segment; (2) a strategy for positioning the resort; and (3) the four P's.

VOCABULARY

For important terms in this case, see the Vocabulary list for Case 10: Penetrating the Market with Long-range Golf Clubs and Bags on pages 95 – 96.

Industrial Pollution: Charting Pollution and Proposing Solutions

CULTURAL BACKGROUND: RELATIONS BETWEEN BUSINESS AND ENVIRONMENTALISTS

Environmental issues can be very sensitive, especially from the point of view of business and industry. Thus, an investigator may not receive full cooperation in the attempt to uncover material. Most countries do have environmental organizations that can provide useful information. However, due to the sensitivity of the situation described in this case, be careful not to antagonize local businesses while at the same time trying to obtain the information necessary to solve the case.

CASE

This is an extension of the case Northern Electrical Services vs. the Environmentalists (Case 6), and the knowledge you gained in solving that case can be applied here. In this case, you are to play the role of an environmentalist group investigating industrial pollution in your area. Begin by targeting one of the major industrial polluters in your area to find out the extent and type of air and water pollution emitted from their company. Local environmental groups can often be helpful in providing this information. Check on whether this company is exceeding nationally set limits (if your country has national standards) or emitting significant amounts of pollutants (in the event that your country does not have national standards), and find out if its management has been warned about their infractions. If they have been warned, find out why they have resisted making the required improvements. If the company does exceed nationally set limits (or emits large amounts of air and/or water pollution), make an estimate of the impact on the health of the local residents. This may be difficult to determine accurately, as it is difficult to isolate the effect of one company's emissions from the total amount of pollution. However, once you have determined the type of pollutants emitted by the targeted factory, you can make an educated guess as to the effects on the health of the local population by seeing if disorders associated with those pollutants are prevalent in your area. Once again, local environmentalist groups can provide valuable information. Often, health studies have already been conducted.

POINTS FOR DISCUSSION

1. Which companies are the major polluters in your area?
2. Have they made any progress in reducing their pollution recently? If so, how have they done so? If not, why not?
3. What can be done to make these companies more environmentally responsible?

CASE ACTIVITIES

Preparing and Presenting Environmental Issues

The environmentalist group should use graphs to present the national standards (or accepted international standards, if your country has no national standards) compared with the company's emissions. These graphs should show incidences of illness (such as cancer, spontaneous abortions, and asthma) which could be associated with the pollutants emitted by the company that you have targeted and compare the number of these incidences with the national average. If there is a significant difference between the national and local averages, be prepared to present and explain this discrepancy.

At the same time that the environmentalist group is preparing a presentation of the amount and effects of the pollution emitted by the targeted company, a second group should prepare the role of management of the same company. They should prepare a defense of their present emission practices. They should also try to guess what improvements the environmentalist group is going to recommend and estimate the costs of these improvements, based on information provided by environmental groups, state environmental agencies, producers of environmental clean-up equipment, or the company's management itself. They should prepare a negotiation position that will include:

1. A statement of their feelings of civic responsibility toward the local community and what they are doing to fulfill their pledge of civic responsibility.
2. An estimation of the costs of installing equipment to meet the emission standards expected to be proposed by the consultant group.
3. The future of the company if they are forced to cover the costs of reducing the amount of pollution emitted from their facilities. You can describe several possible scenarios, based on the costs per percentage of clean-up and the impact on your company's finances. For example,
    a) To remove 90 percent of the sulfur dioxide from our emissions will require equipment at a cost of $X and will have the following impact on our company's finances. . . .
    b) To remove 95 percent of the sulfur dioxide from our emissions will require. . . .

Presentation

The case will involve the presentation of the environmentalist group's findings to the management group. The environmentalist group will graphically represent the following findings:

1. The amount and type of water and air pollution emitted by the company in question (an educated guess).
2. A comparison with accepted standards (either national or recognized international standards).
3. An estimation of the impact of these emissions on the health of the local population (including a commentary linking local incidence of illness to these pollutants, if the incidence of these illnesses significantly exceeds the national average).
4. Recommendations to the company as to what they should do to reduce the amount of pollution emanating from their company and, if possible, the costs of these procedures.

After the environmentalist group presents its findings, the management group can respond on the basis of the three points mentioned on page 104 (a statement of their sense of civic responsibility, an estimate of the costs of reducing pollution, and the impact on the finances of the company). They can choose a hard-line response, suggesting that they are already doing enough and that any increased expenses may force them to consider closing the factory. Or they may make a more flexible response, trying to meet the environmentalist group halfway. Management's response should lead to a discussion between the two groups. It is impossible to know where that discussion will lead, but if the environmentalist group is not satisfied with the result, they may suggest sanctions (such as fines and the like) that could be levied against the company to force them to comply with accepted standards.

Two groups will be chosen to present, one representing management and one representing the environmentalists. These two groups will be chosen at the last minute, so all groups must be prepared to present. The remaining groups' members can ask questions of those presenting after the initial presentations have been made.

LANGUAGE MASTERY EXERCISE

Tone: Confrontation versus Mutuality

The tone of the meeting between the environmentalists and the business management could be either one of *confrontation*, in which the environmentalists demand and management makes counterthreats, or one of *mutuality*, in which the two sides attempt to arrive at a solution. The sentences below will help you develop the vocabulary to deal with either situation. Practice them in pairs until you feel confident in their use. One student should read the first response (that of the environmentalists) and test whether the second student makes an appropriate response.

Confrontation

1. ENVIRONMENTALISTS (E): We demand an immediate cleanup.
      MANAGEMENT (M): You realize that such expenses will cause our factory to become unprofitable, thus forcing its closing.
2. E: You realize that your company is the major polluter in this area.
   M: Can you show us conclusive proof that *we*, rather than another company, are the major polluter?
3. E: If you do not install cleaning systems in your smokestacks, we will block the entrance to your factory.
   M: Have you considered the impact of your actions on the local economy and the possible reaction among the workers at the factory?
4. E: You are using loss of jobs to create fear among the local population and avoid your responsibility to the community.
   M: We are showing responsibility to the local community by providing many well-paid jobs.
5. E: You are the greatest health threat to our community.
   M: Studies we have undertaken show that we are not exceeding accepted limits on emissions.

Mutuality

Responses to environmentalists' claims can also be met with a sense of having a mutual interest in cleaning up the environment, as expressed by the following responses.

   In this pair work exercise, the student representing the environmentalists should make a claim or demand and the student representing management should respond in a manner geared toward reaching a compromise solution. After the student playing the role of management has made his or her offer, the student playing the role of the environmentalists should respond to it. Use some of the following expressions or develop your own responses.

   We are prepared to . . .
   We are willing to . . .
   Would the following be acceptable . . . ?
   We have no objection provided that . . .
   We can meet you halfway and are willing to offer . . .
   We feel that a solution that would be mutually beneficial is . . .

WRITING: NEWSPAPER ARTICLE

The material presented in your oral presentation will be written up in the form of a newspaper article to the local newspaper. This article should include the following:

1. A brief statement of management's position.
2. A brief statement of the environmentalists' position and demands.
3. A summary of the results of the meeting (Was a compromise reached, or does it look like the factory will be closed down and so on).

VOCABULARY

See the Vocabulary list in Case 6: Northern Electrical Services vs. the Environmentalists on pages 57 – 59.

INTERNATIONAL

TRADE

Competing Internationally

CULTURAL BACKGROUND: BRITISH COMPETITIVENESS IN BUSINESS

Because this case involves four to six countries, most of which will be chosen by you, the students, it is not possible to provide a complete cultural background. In fact, an analysis of the cultural background and how it affects the competitiveness of the chosen company is part of the task of this case. However, to give an idea of what this analysis involves, several factors that may impact on companies in Great Britain can be noted. There is a strong sense of class and noticeable class divisions in Great Britain, which may result in conflicts between management and workers or may result in strikes that will reduce productivity. This class division may also influence management's attitude toward its workers and its managerial philosophy and style. Management may be less democratic, and decision making may be more centralized at the top, leading to a top-down (more authoritarian) managerial style. This may be met by a more confrontational attitude on the part of the workers and resistance to changes brought about by managerial decisions based on changing market conditions. British workers have traditionally been less productive than their European counterparts, although Britain has made progress in this area during recent years.

Another cultural factor of importance is the English educational system (note that the Scottish system is different). Two-thirds of English pupils leave school at the age of sixteen; the English system does not emphasize technical education and has a poorly developed apprentice system. This may lead to a poorly educated resource pool. In addition, the school system reflects the class division mentioned above. Many of the top leaders in English politics and business have attended exclusive private schools and then gone on to elite universities, such as Oxford and Cambridge, where they have not studied business subjects. As a result, they have often had little contact with the people they will manage and have not developed an understanding of them nor the interpersonal skills needed to deal with them. In addition, these leaders often develop a very conservative and risk-avoiding view of life and business, which can greatly limit their entrepreneurial spirit.

These are just a few examples of how culture affects business conditions and thus a country's competitiveness. In addition, one finds individual variations in *company* culture from company to company. It is important to analyze company culture as well, as it has a strong impact on competitiveness. Some important aspects of company culture are:

1. *The company's stated philosophy, how it is conveyed to the employees, and to what degree it is followed in the company's daily activities.* The philosophy should include information about managerial philosophy and decision-making practices (democratic or authoritarian, decentralized or centralized).

2. *How the company's management views its workers and what it does to increase job satisfaction.* This is often reflected in how decentralized the decision-making process is and the efforts the company makes to educate and upgrade the skills of its workers.

3. *The degree of information sharing between management and workers.* This is needed so that company goals are shared and so that workers can participate in shaping these goals.

4. *The company's equipment and interior design, which reflect management's attitude toward their products and those who produce them.* Are production facilities modern enough to efficiently produce *state of the art* products (the most advance products possible)? Are the facilities pleasant and healthy, reflecting management's concern for the job satisfaction and health of its workers?

CASE

Recent decades of steadily declining market shares have shown British manufacturers that British industrial dominance is a thing of the past. British manufacturers assumed that their position as market leaders, established before World War II, would go unchallenged, but they have seen that position erode steadily. Faced with the consequences of European unification, such as the *four freedoms* (the free flow of capital, goods, services, and work force), the British economy is likely to become even more vulnerable to the threats posed by the French, Germans, Italians, and Spanish. Thus, the National Economic Development Council has called a seminar to look at the future of British manufacturing. The purpose is to analyze the present state of one industry sector of British manufacturing, whether it be automobiles, steel, electronics, or whatever. The sector to be analyzed and the British company to be used in this case should be chosen by the class.

POINTS FOR DISCUSSION

Discuss some or all of the following factors, stating how and to what degree they impact on a company's ability to compete internationally:

1. Production costs
2. Human resource pool

3. Product quality

4. Research and development

5. Governmental policy (tax, regulation, support, and import restrictions, and so on)

6. Capital costs and the access to capital

7. Impact of exchange rates

8. Use of information technology and computer-assisted design to more rapidly adapt to changing world markets

9. Use of logistical strategies, such as just-in-time delivery, to cut costs

10. Use of joint ventures and coalitions to develop a synergy effect

11. Use of international marketing strategies

12. Organizational structure and its impact on competitiveness

CASE ACTIVITIES

Researching International Trade

This is an open-ended case in which you must research the subject in order to solve the case. After choosing one representative British company in one industry, choose the major competitors in each of three to five other EU (European Union) countries. Make a comparative study of the British company in regard to some or all of the factors mentioned in the Points for Discussion above. Based on this comparison, make a prognosis for the possible future success of the British company and a list of changes that will need to be made in order for this company to succeed in the EU.

This case should be presented in several sessions. First, the British company should be presented by a group whose presentation will include some or all of the areas just described. In the next session, the other groups will present their companies and compare them with the British company in these areas. In the final session, the group presenting the British company will present the future strategy for competition, taking into account what they have learned about the competitors. Naturally, they will have to propose changes in the company and the means of carrying out these changes. There must be enough time between each session to allow the groups adequate time to prepare.

LANGUAGE MASTERY EXERCISES

Terms for Comparison: Comparatives and Superlatives

In this case you will be comparing companies. You will use the *comparative* form of adjectives when comparing two companies, and the *superlative* form when comparing more than two companies:

Comparatives

Comparatives are used to compare two subjects.

Adjective	Comparative Form	Example
good	better	Our products are better than theirs.
bad	worse	Their profits were worse than expected.

Use *-er* endings to make regular one- or two-syllable adjectives into comparative adjectives. For example, the comparative form of *smart* is *smarter:*

Barbara is *smarter* than Joe.

Use *less* or *more*, plus the adjective, to make comparative adjectives from regular adjectives with three or more syllables. For example, the comparative form of *complicated* is *more* (or *less*) *complicated:*

Their system is *more complicated* than ours.
Our system is *less complicated* than theirs.

Note: Use *as . . . as* when making equal comparisons.

Our products are *as* good *as* theirs.

Exercise: Using Comparatives

Using the following nouns and adjectives, make sentences comparing two companies.

Examples:

Noun	Adjective
1. costs	high

Our costs were higher than theirs.

Noun	Adjective
company	profitable (*equal*)

Our company is as profitable as Company X.

Noun	Adjective
1. profits	high
2. costs	low
3. workers	productive (*equal*)
4. designers	creative (*equal*)
5. employees	highly educated
6. technology	highly developed
7. production costs	expensive
8. financial position	solid
9. design	advanced (Use the word *less* in the sentence.)
10. prices	competitive (Use the word *less* in the sentence.)

Superlatives

Superlatives are used to compare three or more subjects.

Adjective	Superlative Form	Example
good	best	Our company is the best of the three.
bad	worst	Their products are the worst of the five displayed.

Use *-st* endings to make regular one- or two-syllable adjectives into comparative adjectives. For example, the superlative form of *fast* is *fastest:*

> This is the *fastest* machinery on the market.

Use *least* or *most*, plus the adjective, to make superlative adjectives from regular adjectives with three or more syllables. For example, the superlative form of *impressive* is *most* (or *least*) *impressive:*

> The *least impressive* product was made by Company X.
> The *most impressive* product was made by Company Y.

Note: In making equal comparisons of three or more subjects, use the same form as used in comparing two subjects.

> Our products are *as* good *as* all of our competitors' products.

Exercise: Using Superlatives

Using the adjectives and nouns in the Exercise on page 112, make sentences in the superlative.

WRITING: REPORT ON COMPETITIVE POSITION

Each group will write a separate report stating the competitive position of their company and suggesting necessary changes to improve that competitive position. This report should be complete with a vocabulary list of terms relevant to this case and their definitions.

VOCABULARY

brand, *n.*   The name associated with a specific product, such as Coca-Cola, Ford, Phillips.

business climate, *n.*   The general conditions for doing business and producing goods in a country, including such factors as government regulations and support, interest rates, and union-management relations.

coalitions, *n.*   Formal, long-term alliances between firms that link aspects of their business without actually entering into a merger.

consumer confidence, *n.*   The confidence consumers have in a company's products, which is often reflected in consumer loyalty (the degree to which a consumer will purchase the same brand when making new purchases).

economies of scale, *n.*   The advantages gained by large-scale production, which reduces per unit cost of products.

EU, *n.*   The European Union.

job security, *n.*   The likelihood that a worker will not be laid off (that is, have his or her employment terminated, due to a lack of work).

joint venture, *n.*   A partnership formed by two or more companies to cooperate on some special business activity.

just-in-time logistics, *n.*   Delivering goods to customers directly, based on computerized models, to save warehousing costs.

loyalty, *n.*   A relationship of trust and concern, developed between employers and employees, that causes workers to feel secure in their jobs and to make a maximum effort.

market mix, *n.*   The combination of the four P's (product, price, promotion, and place) that best meets the needs of the consumer.

market research, *n.*   Research done to determine the conditions and the potentials of a market.

market shares, *n.*   The percentage of the total market that a product achieves in a given market.

positioning, *n.*   Meeting the needs of a market by (a) developing a new product, (b) altering an existing one, or (c) changing the image of an existing product through advertising.

product differentiation, *n.*   Any difference, real or imaginary, that sets a product apart from competitors' products and, it is hoped, makes it more attractive to the consumer.

production costs, *n.*   The costs of producing goods, including fixed costs (such as factories), direct costs (such as labor), material costs, and capital costs (such as interest on loans).

production time, *n.*   The length of time it takes to produce a product.

productivity, *n.*   The average amount of goods produced by a worker in a given amount of time. The higher the productivity, the lower the cost per unit.

prognosis, *n.*   A prediction about future business conditions and potential markets and sales.

quality, *n.*   How good or bad a product is. Ways of evaluating quality include *customer satisfaction studies* (which indicate how satisfied customers are with the product) and *recall* (the number of products that have been recalled due to mistakes in production, which must be corrected).

recall, *n.*   Having to call in products to correct mistakes in production. A high recall percentage raises questions about the quality of a product.

R & D (Research and Development), *n.*   Studies involving the discovery of new potential products and the development of the actual product.

recognition factor, *n.*   The degree of familiarity among consumers of a company's brands.

synergy, *n.*   The effect gained by merging the strengths of two or more companies.

target market, *n.*   After segmentation, the segment (a part of the total market) at which a company chooses to aim their product.

REFERENCES

The following two works should provide you with the information and vocabulary to solve this case. If these textbooks are not available in your library, look for other textbooks on competitive analysis.

Oster, Sharon M. *Modern Competitive Analysis*. Oxford: Oxford University Press, 1990.

Porter, Michael. *Competition in Global Industries*. Boston: Harvard Business School Press, 1986.

BUSINESS

ORGANIZATION

AND MANAGEMENT

Saturn: Can American Automobile Manufacturers Compete with the Japanese?

CULTURAL BACKGROUND: AMERICAN AND JAPANESE BUSINESS CULTURES

This case provides the opportunity to analyze two business cultures and discover their strengths and weaknesses. Solving it will give you insight into differences in human resource policies, including the relation between management and workers, attitudes toward research and development, and the ability to react quickly to changing markets and production techniques and their impact on productivity. It is a classic case providing a look into the business cultures of two leading industrial nations — useful information for future businesspersons like yourselves.

CASE

In your studies, you have undoubtedly encountered the problem American manufacturers have had competing with the Japanese. Here is a chance to use your theoretical knowledge. When General Motors (GM) decided to produce the Saturn model, they took the radical step of starting a whole new company and factory outside of the parent company. This could be seen as an admission of defeat, in that GM seemed to be saying that they simply could not produce a competitive car within the present company framework, due to its bureaucratic rigidity and all that it entailed in terms of impeding changes in engineering, production, and human resource policy. In addition, this decision could have been an admission, explicit or implicit, of the many failings of American automobile manufacturing, not only at GM but across the board. Comparative figures from the time when the idea of Saturn was developed (1983) show the competitive advantages that the Japanese enjoyed.* In 1979, the market share captured by Japanese automobiles was 17 percent; three years later, in 1982, it had grown to 30 percent.

Cost differentials between Japanese and American automobiles show a competitive advantage in favor of the Japanese in 1983, the year this case takes place:

---

*Figures source: William J. Abernathy et al. *Industrial Renaissance: Producing a Competitive Future for America*. New York: Basic Books, 1983.

	Japan	USA
Hourly wage rate (average) + benefits	$11.91	$23.31
Total production costs per vehicle (average)	$4,211	$6,520
Capacity utilization level	95%	85%
Capacity adjusted costs	$4,363	$7,285

The cost of American cars averaged $2,922 more than Japanese cars for comparative models.

In terms of customer satisfaction, Japanese automobiles enjoyed this advantage: Approximately 75 percent of American car owners, versus 93 percent of Japanese car owners, said that they would purchase the same make of car again.

Management's attitudes towards their work force can be reflected in layoff figures, in that these figures represent human resource policy and consideration for the workers' welfare. In 1983, the Japanese no-layoff policy resulted in virtually no layoffs, while in the years between 1980 and 1984, Ford and Chrysler laid off 40 percent of their workers, and GM laid off 17 percent of its workers. One can hypothesize that workers who feel secure in their jobs will feel greater loyalty to the company, and that loyalty will be reflected in their job performance.

The figures listed here illustrate some of the problems American automobile producers faced in 1983. Such problems required a change in their approach to producing automobiles. Following are some of the problems that the Saturn project attempted to solve (and with which this case will deal).

Engineering

Can American engineers produce a quality, gas-efficient car that can be assembled in a competitive number of working hours? Can engineering be responsive to consumers' needs, or do they expect the consumer to adapt to the engineers' product?

Take for example the complaint of American automobile makers that the Japanese market is restrictive, thus making market penetration difficult. While this is true, it is also true that the American cars exported to Japan have had the steering wheel on the left, as in American cars. However, the Japanese drive on the left side of the road and need the steering wheel on the right. Granted, American car manufacturers are finally producing cars with the steering wheels on the right for export. But how many years did it take them to adapt?

Another case of poor adaptation to consumers' demands is the slow response of the American automobile industry to the oil crisis in the 1970s. American companies kept on producing gas guzzlers long after it became apparent that the market was calling for more fuel-efficient cars. This left the door open for the Japanese penetration into the U. S. car market.

Then there is the question of quality. Japanese cars generally led the list of cars eliciting the least complaints from customers, whereas American cars more often fell nearer the bottom of the list. American cars have made some progress in this area in recent years. But this progress has been slow, and American-made cars have developed a bad reputation that their manufacturers are now struggling to overcome. When you discuss engineering, you are going to have to come up with ways for American automobile companies to be more consumer- and quality-oriented.

Production

According to a recent television report, it takes GM an average of 44 working hours to assemble a car, while Ford and Japanese automobile makers take less than half that time. In designing your production facility, you will have to take this into account and, based on approaches from either Saturn or other successful car manufacturing plants, suggest ways of cutting production time.

Human Resources

There are glaring gaps between the job security and family loyalty approach of Japanese employers and the periodic layoffs and plant-closing approach of American automobile employers. Does GM care about their employees? If not, will they be able to produce quality cars until they *do* start caring about the people that design and build them? You will have to design a human resource policy that is more responsive to the needs of employees, in hopes of increasing employees' motivation, which will in turn lead to greater output and quality.

Organizational Structure

GM has been criticized for its deep and hierarchical structure, which makes the company too bureaucratic and, in turn, leads to a slowness in responding to market trends. Recent critics have wondered why it has taken GM so long to respond to obvious changes. Some analysts believe the nation's large firms might have avoided recent traumatic cost cutting if they had been more responsive to the fundamental competitive challenges of the last two decades. Perhaps creating separate, smaller companies with flatter organizational structures (i.e., fewer levels) like that of the Saturn project is the way of the future. In any case, you will have to set up a flatter, more responsive organizational structure for the Saturn project that can respond to changes in the market more rapidly than the present deep structure at GM.

POINTS FOR DISCUSSION

1. Discuss in detail recent developments in the competition and cooperation between American and Japanese automobile manufacturers. Do recent improvements in American competitiveness reflect improvements in engineering, production, organizational structure, and human resource policy or are these improvements simply a result of the strength of Japanese currency, which makes Japanese cars too expensive?

2. Discuss whether the American automobile producers will be able to recapture

some of the market shares they have lost to the Japanese and what they will have to do to recapture these shares.

CASE ACTIVITIES

Corporate Organization

The purpose of this case is to give you insight into problems faced by large corporations and the opportunity to work on solutions to these problems in English. In this case, you will form task forces to discuss the areas mentioned above and outline a strategy for the establishing of the company to produce Saturns. Your meeting will consist of two representatives from each of the four departments suggested above: Engineering, Production, Human Resources, and Management. There will be as many task forces as the size of your class allows. After each task force has reached conclusions concerning the four areas mentioned above, compare notes in a classroom discussion, with each task force presenting and defending its conclusions and answering questions from the other task forces. In advance of the meeting, all members of each section should meet separately and discuss aspects of their area's problem. Thus, they will prepare in advance of the meeting. Diagrammed, the process will look like this:

PHASE 1: PREPARATION

Engineering	Human Resources	Management	Production
Student A	Student E	Student I	Student M
Student B	Student F	Student J	Student N
Student C	Student G	Student K	Student O
Student D	Student H	Student L	Student P

PHASE 2: TASK FORCE MEETINGS

Meeting 1: Students A, B, E, F, I, J, M, N
Meeting 2: Students C, D, G, H, K, L, O, P

This structure assumes that you have 16 students. If you have more students, you can have three or more task forces.

This is an open-ended case, which means that all the information necessary to solve the case is *not* provided here. Thus, you will have to research the case. Fortunately, the Saturn project drew much media attention, so you should find plenty of material in newspapers, magazines, and so on.

This case provides an opportunity for creative information-gathering techniques and case solutions. The engineers in the case should address the questions of design and quality that are available in Saturn brochures. The Production people should discuss ways of rationalizing assembly and present drawings of production facilities. Human Resources should outline a policy that is in line with employees' needs. Management should propose an organizational structure that is more responsive to employee suggestions (including open channels of communication and a flatter structure, for example). In addition, this group should discuss a more decentralized decision-making system and an organization that is more responsive to changes in the market.

The task forces should discuss solutions in the four areas mentioned above and prepare a presentation. *Although you will be referring to articles and other materials about the development of the actual Saturn project, you should discuss this case as if it were 1983 and* you *were developing the project.* Thus, you can make reference to the failings of GM and propose your solutions as a remedy for GM's problems.

When the task forces have come to a conclusion and have a strategy for the establishing of Saturn, their conclusions should be presented to the class, along with diagrams of (a) car designs, (b) more efficient assembly plants, and (c) a flatter, more responsive organizational structure. The task forces should also present statements concerning management and personnel policy and ways of insuring quality and production efficiency. Each task force should present and defend their conclusions. The other class members can ask questions and criticize the presenting task force's conclusions, which should lead to lively discussion.

LANGUAGE MASTERY EXERCISES

See the exercises on pages 111–113.

WRITING: GROUP PROJECT/REPORT

The information from the oral presentation should be written up in the form of a report. As this case is fairly advanced, the report can be considered a group project term paper, which will receive a grade.

VOCABULARY

See the Vocabulary list in Case 13 ("Competing Internationally") on pages 113–115.

REFERENCES

Also refer to articles in *Business Week*, the *Wall Street Journal*, and *Fortune*.

Daft, Richard L. *Organizational Theory and Design*. St. Paul, Minn: West Publishing, 1992.

Oster, Sharon M. *Modern Competitive Analysis*. Oxford: Oxford University Press, 1990.

Porter, Michael. *Competition in Global Industries*. Boston: Harvard Business School Press, 1986.

Appendix 1
TELEPHONE
ENGLISH

The majority of your communication in English will be over the telephone. In fact, in international trade it is possible to have business relationships for years without ever seeing the people with whom you are dealing. It is through the telephone that you project an impression of yourself and the company you represent. Thus, it is extremely important that you master the skills necessary to communicate well over the telephone, which is the purpose of this Appendix.

The activities in this Appendix will make you aware of the subtle differences in communication that make a big difference in the impression you create. Not being aware of these differences can result in your seeming rude or arrogant, unsophisticated or not service-minded. It can take no more than saying "I want" instead of "I would like to" to create a bad impression. In addition, there is the cultural element that must also be understood in order to communicate effectively with native English speakers. First, you must be made aware of a standard form that English telephone conversations often have. Second, you should be aware of two extremely important cultural values that must be expressed: politeness and service-mindedness. So let us take a look at these elements and then practice them until they become second nature.

ANSWERING A BUSINESS TELEPHONE CALL

Seven Steps

Following is a list of seven steps you may use to answer the telephone in a business setting.

1. GREETING

> Hello.
> Good morning.
> Good afternoon.

The greeting is optional and would mainly be used by switchboard operators (for example, *Good morning, General Foods*). However, it is appropriate if you are sure the call is coming from outside the company.

2. IDENTIFICATION

Accounting, David Warner speaking.

3. OFFER OF HELP

May I help you?
How may I help you?

This is also optional but recommended when dealing with customers. Thus, if you work in customer service, customer relations, or sales, offering help would be appropriate.

4. EXCHANGE OF INFORMATION

This is the core of the telephone conversation, in which information is exchanged, requests are made, meetings are arranged, and so on. It is here that you can show your sophistication by being informative, polite, and service-minded.

5. CONFIRMATION OF MESSAGE

If the caller has made a request, if a meeting date has been set, or if something has been decided, repeat it to be sure that both parties have understood the same thing or that the request is clear. This will help avoid misunderstandings. Confirmation of the message is expected as part of a conversation by English-speaking people, and it makes your telephone manners seem more sophisticated.

6. CONFIRMATION OF ACTION

You confirm that you will do what is requested or what has been decided. If time permits, you should follow this up by confirming your intended action in writing.

7. CLOSING

"Goodbye" is the standard closing, but you can make a good final impression in this call by adding something polite or service-minded, such as "If you have any other questions, don't hesitate to call," or "Thank you for calling. I'm looking forward to our meeting."

Now let's walk through a standard telephone call using the seven steps.

BJ: Good morning. Macintosh Customer Service, Bill Jenkins speaking. How may I help you? [Steps 1–3]

DJ: My name is Dick Johnson. I just bought a Macintosh LC II with Systems 7, but I didn't get the operations manual.

BJ: Oh, that's strange. It should have been included in the package. It's called Macintosh Reference 7. However, that's easy to solve. I'll send you a copy by UPS (United Parcel Service). You should get it in a couple of days. What's your address, Mr. Johnson? [Note that an American employee might refer to this customer as "Dick." The use of first names is very common in the United States, but much less common in Great Britain.]

DJ: It's 515 Wilson Avenue, Kingston, Rhode Island 02881. [Step 4]

BJ: Let me repeat that, Mr. Johnson. That was 515 Wilson Avenue, Kingston, Rhode Island 02881. [Step 5]

BJ: I'll put a copy of Macintosh Reference 7 in the mail and you should get it by Friday. [Steps 5 and 6] Is there anything else I can do for you? [A sign of service-mindedness.]

DJ: No. That should do it.

BJ: All right, but if you have any other questions, don't hesitate to call. [Once again, service-mindedness.] Goodbye.

DJ: Goodbye.

Telephone Etiquette

As you can see, it takes so little to make a good impression, but it makes all the difference in the world. So let's look at some standard phrases that will help.

Be Polite

Adding "please" always creates a polite tone, especially along with the conditional "could" and "would." Compare "Would you please repeat that" with "What?", or "I would like to speak to. . ." with "I want to speak to . . . ," or "I would appreciate your sending me" with "Send me. . . ." In each case, the first form is polite and the second is blunt. Also, do not forget "thank you" and "please." These phrases add another polite dimension. "Convenient" is another word that adds politeness and consideration to your conversation. For example, when planning a meeting, you might say, "What is a convenient time for you?" Or if you propose a time, you might phrase it, "Is that convenient for you?" The key is remembering how you would want to be treated on the telephone and using your own expectations as your guidelines.

Be Service-minded

This is another attitude that will create a good impression. One tip is that if a caller has a problem, feel that it is your goal to solve it. For example, a positive response might be, "Yes, I understand the problem. Let me investigate a couple of possibilities, and I'll get back to you." Compare such a response with "I really do not know what we can do about that." If you do not have an immediate answer, do not just give up. Make an investigation, and see if you can find an answer. Finally, always stress that you will get back to the caller soon. And do it!

Be Informative

Don't force people to ask questions. Be forthcoming. When you do get a question, give a complete answer. Try to imagine what information the caller would want if he or she knew it were available. For example, let's say that a customer calls to ask about material on an information system, and there is a new system just out on the market. You should say, "Are you aware that we just put System 7 on the market?" and then go into a brief description of its advantages. You can close by saying, "I'll send you brochures on both systems so that you can choose which is best for you." Or let's say someone calls for your office mate, who is in a meeting. You can answer, "Mr. Johnson is in a meeting" or "Mr. Johnson is in a meeting. I expect him back at two o'clock. Would you like to leave a message?" Obviously the latter response is much more professional.

Practice

In the following conversations, practice the seven steps and the telephone etiquette suggested above.

Taking a Message

You receive a call for your office mate who is not in the office. In a polite fashion, take a message. After you have done this once, reverse the roles and do it again.

KEY PHRASES

Mr. Johnson's telephone, Peter Smith speaking.

Mr. Johnson (1) is away from his desk, (2) just stepped out for a moment, (3) is in a meeting, (4) is not in today, (5) is on a business trip. Would you like to leave a message? [Another possibility is "Can I help you?"]

Mr. Johnson is on another line. Would you like to hold or would you like to leave a message? Would you like him to call you back?

Remember to repeat the message to confirm it and then confirm that you will do what the caller requests. For example, "Thank you, Mr. Williams. I'll have Mr. Johnson call you at 790-8978 as soon as he comes in." If you want the caller to repeat a name, say "Excuse me, could you repeat that?" or "Could you spell that, please?" In confirming the caller's number, you could say, "That was 790-8978."

Arranging a Meeting

Call and arrange a meeting.

KEY PHRASES

Let's set up a meeting.

When is it convenient for you?

Wednesday is most convenient for me.

Let me check my schedule/calendar.

How about two o'clock? *Or* Is two o'clock all right/convenient?

Using the key phrases above, call to arrange a meeting. After you have done this once, reverse roles and do it again.

Booking an Airline Ticket

Call and book an airline ticket. The airline agent will need information such as time and day of departure, class, smoking or non-smoking section, and time and day of return. The traveler will want to know price, seating (window or aisle seat), and whether it is a direct or nonstop flight.

KEY WORDS AND PHRASES

> Departing
>
> Arriving
>
> Flight number
>
> Tourist, business, or first class
>
> Direct or nonstop
>
> Check-in time

Using these words or phrases, book a ticket with an airline agent. After you have done this once, reverse roles and do it again. When you play the agent, be sure to confirm all details about the ticket.

Dealing with a Complaint

Invent two situations in which a customer has a complaint. Play out the telephone conversations so that both of you play each role (customer and customer service representative) once. Dealing with complaints requires the utmost in language sophistication to avoid losing a customer. In this situation, you must calm the customer down, solve the problem, and reestablish good will.

KEY PHRASES

> I'm sorry that this has inconvenienced you.
>
> I'll get over there right away. *Or* I'll send a serviceperson immediately.
>
> That almost never happens, but we will have someone there within an hour.
>
> I'm sorry our delivery was late. We had a mix-up. But I'll see that it never happens again.
>
> I'll see what I can do and get back to you immediately.
>
> I'm afraid that there is nothing we can do at the moment. But I'll get back to you as soon as I can, say in a day or two.

You can invent as many situations as you feel are useful until you feel comfortable on the phone. Possible situations include reserving a table at a restaurant, selling a product over the telephone, or informing a customer that his or her account is in arrears (i.e., payment is overdue).

Following are more key words and phrases for using the telephone:

> to dial
>
> to transfer

to connect you

to be put on hold

to call back

to page (*v.*)

radio pager (*n.*)

switchboard

operator (*n.*)

information (*n.*) (British: *directory inquiries*)

local call (*n.*)

long-distance call (*n.*) (British: *trunk call*)

telephone number (*n.*)

extension (*n.*)

I'm sorry, you have the wrong number.

Use the above words to fill in the blanks in the following telephone conversations:

OPERATOR: This is _____ . What city please?

MS. JONES: Boston. The telephone _____ for A. J. Smiths.

OPERATOR: Their _____ is 678-8897.

MS. JONES: Is that a _____ or _____ call from a 665 exchange?

OPERATOR: It's in the same area, so it's a _____ call.

MS. JONES: Thank you, Operator.

SWITCHBOARD OPERATOR AT A. J. SMITHS: A. J. Smiths. Good morning.

MS. JONES: Mr. Johnson at _____ 255, please.

SWITCHBOARD OPERATOR: Just a moment. I'll _____ you.

MR. WILLIAMS: Accounting, Mr. Williams.

MS. JONES: Excuse me. Is this _____ 255?

MR. WILLIAMS: No, I'm sorry. This is 253.

MS. JONES: Oh, the _____ connected me with the _____ .

MR. WILLIAMS: No problem. I'll _____ your call to 255.

MS. DICKSON: Mr. Johnson's telephone.

MS. JONES: Is Mr. Johnson in? _____

Ms. Dickson: No he isn't, but I can ＿＿＿＿＿＿＿＿ him.
He has a ＿＿＿＿＿＿＿＿ . Oh, excuse me.
Mr. Johnson is in the next office. I can hear
his voice, but he's on another line. Do you
want me to put you ＿＿＿＿＿＿＿＿ or do
you want to ＿＿＿＿＿＿＿ later?

Ms. Jones: You can put me ＿＿＿＿＿＿＿＿ .

The Alphabet

In taking or giving messages, it is essential to know the English alphabet because
many names and addresses must be spelled. So here is an alphabet review to help
master the sounds of each letter:

[ei]	[i:]	[e]	[ai]	[u:]	[owe]
a (bay)	b (be)	f (le*ft*)	i (I)	q (cue)	o(go)
h (a + ch)	c (sea)	l (*el*ectric)	y (why)	u (you)	
j (jay)	d (*dee*d)	m (the*m*)		w (double you)	
k (Kay)	e (m*e*)	n (m*e*n)			
	g (gee)	x (*e*xit)			
	p (pea)	z (zee) (British: zed)			
	t (tea)				
	v (vee)				

r (ba*r*)   s (me*ss*)

After you have practiced the sounds as a class, break into pairs. One person
should spell personal and company names and addresses aloud while the other
writes them down. Reverse roles until you both can quickly recognize the words
being spelled and write them down.

Appendix 2

BUSINESS

WRITING

The purpose of this Appendix is to provide you with important tips and a general introduction to the basic components of business writing: format, style, and tone. The material presented here will provide information and models to complete the written exercises in this book that deal with business writing.

BASIC TIPS

1. Ask to see business correspondence in English at the place where you work. This will give you (a) the relevant vocabulary in your profession, and (b) a sense of the format used by your employer.

2. Purchase a handbook for business correspondence. Make sure that the book has examples of different kinds of correspondence, including memos, letters, and reports. The book should also have sample letters for different purposes, such as request for payment, request for information, acknowledgment, cover letter, and so on. The vocabulary for each type of letter is fairly standard; thus, in writing a letter, you can find the type of letter you are writing in your handbook and use that letter's vocabulary as a guide.

3. If at all possible, have someone who is a native English speaker correct the draft of your letter before you write a final draft. This could save you much embarrassment. Also, keep copies of your original draft and the final copy and review them periodically. This will help you see and eliminate the mistakes you made before. You will soon discover that business letters follow a formula consisting of phrases like the following:

   In response to your letter of . . .

   We regret that we cannot . . .

   We look forward to . . .

   You will soon learn these phrases by studying a handbook for business correspondence and by having your original drafts proofread and corrected by a native English speaker.

FORMAT

Letters

There are three basic letter formats: (1) *block style*, in which all the lines begin at the left-hand margin; (2) *modified block style*, in which the dateline, the complimentary close, and the sender's name and title at the end begin in the center of the page; and (3) *indented* (also called *modified block with paragraph indentations*), in which each first line of a new paragraph is indented five spaces and the sender's address and date are placed on the upper right-hand side of the page. Figures A-1 through A-3 give you examples of all three styles.

Letterheads

Most business letters are typed on stationery with a printed address known as the *letterhead*. Thus, the placement of the sender's address will be predetermined.

Dateline

There is a slight difference between the formats of American and British datelines:

American: May 22, 1995
British: 22 May 1995

Inside Address

This is to be typed anywhere from three to twelve lines below the date, depending on the length of your letter. The shorter the letter, the more space there should be between the date and the inside address. Be sure to check the spelling of the name of the person receiving the letter, as well as his or her title and address.

Salutations

The standard salutation for a man is *Dear Mr.* For women, the preferred salutation is *Dear Ms.* In the event that the name of the receiver is unknown, use *Dear Sir* or *Dear Madam*, or *Dear Sir or Madam* if the sex of the receiver is unknown.

Subject

Many business letters begin with *SUBJECT:* or *Re:*, which states the subject of the letter. This aids the reader in knowing what the letter is about without having to read the entire letter.

```
Video Distributors
231 Allen Road
Wakefield, RI 02879


May 22, 199_

David Wilson
Wilson Video
451 Broad Street
Providence, RI 02905

Dear Mr. Wilson:

SUBJECT: Video Distributors' Catalogue for 199_

Thank you very much for your letter of April 22 requesting our 199_
catalogue. Please excuse the delay in sending you the enclosed
catalogue, which resulted from unforeseen problems at the printer.
I am sure you will agree that the catalogue was worth the wait. We
have doubled our holdings from last year by securing an exclusive
contract with Global Video Production. In addition, we have added
new lines of educational and business training videos.

As a means of promoting our new lines of educational and business
training videos, we have a special offer for the remainder of 199_.
Order five educational and/or business videos, and the sixth one is
free. We have designed promotional materials for each category of
video, which we will provide free of charge. We have also compiled a
list of potential customers in your area for each category of video.
Naturally, when you succeed, we succeed, and we are doing our utmost
to insure our mutual success.

We have streamlined our order processing service, which means three-
day delivery upon the receipt of your order. We are looking forward
to a continued profitable business relationship. If you have any
questions, please do not hesitate to call me.

Sincerely yours,



David House
Customer Service Representative

Enclosure
```

Figure A-1 Block style letter

Video Distributors
231 Allen Road
Wakefield, RI 02879

                                May 22, 199_

David Wilson
Wilson Video
451 Broad Street
Providence, RI 02905

Dear Mr. Wilson:

SUBJECT: Video Distributors' Catalogue for 199_

Thank you very much for your letter of April 22 requesting our 199_
catalogue. Please excuse the delay in sending you the enclosed
catalogue, which resulted from unforeseen problems at the printer.
I am sure you will agree that the catalogue was worth the wait. We
have doubled our holdings from last year by securing an exclusive
contract with Global Video Production. In addition, we have added
new lines of educational and business training videos.

As a means of promoting our new lines of educational and business
training videos, we have a special offer for the remainder of 199_.
Order five educational and/or business videos, and the sixth one is
free. We have designed promotional materials for each category of
video, which we will provide free of charge. We have also compiled a
list of potential customers in your area for each category of video.
Naturally, when you succeed, we succeed, and we are doing our utmost
to insure our mutual success.

We have streamlined our order processing service, which means three-
day delivery upon the receipt of your order. We are looking forward
to a continued profitable business relationship. If you have any
questions, please do not hesitate to call me.

                                Sincerely yours,

                                David House
                                Customer Service Representative

Enclosure

Figure A-2   Modified block style letter

```
                                    Video Distributors
                                    231 Allen Road
                                    Wakefield, RI 02879


                                    May 22, 199_

David Wilson
Wilson Video
451 Broad Street
Providence, RI 02905

Dear Mr. Wilson:

         SUBJECT: Video Distributors' Catalogue for 199_

    Thank you very much for your letter of April 22 requesting our
199_ catalogue. Please excuse the delay in sending you the enclosed
catalogue, which resulted from unforeseen problems at the printer.
I am sure you will agree that the catalogue was worth the wait. We
have doubled our holdings from last year by securing an exclusive
contract with Global Video Production. In addition, we have added
new lines of educational and business training videos.
    As a means of promoting our new lines of educational and busi-
ness training videos, we have a special offer for the remainder of
199_. Order five educational and/or business videos, and the sixth
one is free. We have designed promotional materials for each cate-
gory of video, which we will provide free of charge. We have also
compiled a list of potential customers in your area for each cate-
gory of video. Naturally, when you succeed, we succeed, and we are
doing our utmost to insure our mutual success.
    We have streamlined our order processing service, which means
three-day delivery upon the receipt of your order. We are looking
forward to a continued profitable business relationship. If you have
any questions, please do not hesitate to call me.

                                    Sincerely yours,



                                    David House
                                    Customer Service Representative

Enclosure
```

Figure A-3 Indented style letter

Complimentary Closings

These closings can be characterized by their degree of formality:

1. *Less formal:* Sincerely, Sincerely yours, Yours sincerely.
   These are the standard closings for an American business letter. Note that only the first word in the complimentary closing is capitalized.
2. *More formal:* Respectfully yours, Yours respectfully, Yours truly.
   The British tend to be more formal and thus use these complimentary closings more often than Americans do. These are also standard closings for letters beginning with *Dear Sir, Dear Madam,* or *Dear Sir or Madam.*

Office Memorandums

Generally referred to as a *memo,* the office memorandum is the basic form of written communication between company employees and is less formal than a letter. It is used (a) for messages that are complicated, (b) to avoid making unnecessary telephone calls on subjects that are not urgent, and (c) when a record of the communication is necessary. Usually they are brief. Figure A-4 contains the basic elements of an office memo.

Reports

Because there are so many different types of reports, it is not possible to deal fully with the subject of reports in this section. Instead, this section will provide you with a model as a guideline for writing reports.

Title Page

A sample title page is shown in Figure A-5.

```
      TO: William Smith, Chief Shipping Clerk

    FROM: David House, Customer Service Representative

    DATE: June 10, 1994

 SUBJECT: Shipment of Order #3452 to Wilson Video

Order #3452 to Wilson Video was supposed to be sent on June 5, 199_,
in compliance with our three-day delivery policy. Per today's date,
Wilson Video has not received the shipment. Please check the status
of this shipment, and inform me.
```

Figure A-4   Interoffice Memo

```
                          A REPORT
               OF THE NEGOTIATIONS BETWEEN
                    XYZ DISTRIBUTORS
                          AND
               LONG-RANGE GOLF EQUIPMENT, INC.


          Compiled by the XYZ Negotiations Team

            David Williams, Marketing Manager

             Joyce Daniels, Sales Manager

          Connie Smith, Chief Judicial Adviser
```

```
                      July 22, 199_
```

Figure A-5 Title page

Executive Summary

The executive summary is a brief description of the contents of the report, which allows a reader to know if the report is relevant to his or her purposes without having to read the entire thing. It should be typed on a separate page. An example from the report named in the title page (see Figure A-5) is shown in Figure A-6.

Table of Contents

The table of contents is placed after the summary. Prepared after the report is completed, it lists in order the numbers and titles of the sections or chapters in the report and the pages on which they begin. In numbering, you have a choice between the American system of calling the sections *chapters* (for example, *Chapter 1*) or the British system illustrated in Figure A-7. The table of contents should appear on its own page. The American form, using Roman numerals, capital letters, and cardinal numbers, is shown in Figure A-8.

The Body

The body of the report follows the structure given in the table of contents. Each section's title is placed in a heading with the number and capitalized heading (for example, 4.0 The Negotiation). Each subsection is placed in a subheading with the first letter of each word capitalized (for example, 4.1 The Resulting Contract). So a page might begin as shown in Figure A-9.

STYLE AND TONE

The discussion of style cannot be as concrete as that of format because the question of style is determined by company policy as well as personal writing style. To familiarize yourself with a given company's style, review business documents

```
                        EXECUTIVE SUMMARY


        On July 15, 199_, formal negotiations with Long-range were held
   to discuss terms of an eventual contract to distribute Long-range
   golf equipment. This report represents the pre-negotiations segment
   and XYZ's goals and strategies, as well as an assessment of the
   financial benefits of distributing Long-range golf equipment and an
   account of the negotiation process and resulting contact. Also
   included are our assessment of the contract and our recommendation
   on whether to accept the contract.
```

Figure A-6 Executive Summary

```
                        TABLE OF CONTENTS


TITLE PAGE                                                    (i)

TABLE OF CONTENTS                                            (ii)

1.0  EXECUTIVE SUMMARY                                         1

2.0  INTRODUCTION                                             2

3.0  PRE-NEGOTIATION                                          4
     3.1  Our Goals                                           4
          3.1.1  Musts
          3.1.2  Trading Cards
          3.1.3  The Bottom Line
     3.2  An Assessment of the Balance of Power               5
          3.2.1  How Much Do We Need Them?
          3.2.2  How Much Do They Need Us?

4.0  THE NEGOTIATIONS                                          7
     4.1  The Resulting Contract                               8

5.0  AN ASSESSMENT OF THE CONTRACT                            12
     5.1  Our Goals Compared with the Results Achieved        12

6.0  RECOMMENDATION                                           15
```

Figure A-7   Table of Contents, British-style

written in English and talk to the persons responsible for typing the company's correspondence in English. These people have a wealth of information just waiting to be tapped.

However, certain generalizations *can* be made about English style, and these

```
III.  Pre-Negotiation
      A.  Our Goals
          1.  Musts
          2.  Trading Cards
          3.  The Bottom Line
```

Figure A-8   Table of contents, American-style

```
4.0  NEGOTIATIONS
     4.1 The Resulting Contract
     The contract reached contains the following terms . . .
```

Figure A-9 Body of a report

can serve as guidelines. First, English business style is concise. This means your writing should be brief and concrete. For example, the French expression *Je vous prie de bien vouloir* is translated as *please* in English. Certain cultures have a tendency to be more ornate, even metaphorical, in their writing style. But there is little room for poetic devices in English business style. Stick to the facts and keep it brief. Note the following examples of wordiness and accompanying suggestions for how to be more concise:

Wordy	**Concise**
the question as to whether	whether (the question whether)
there is no doubt but that	no doubt (doubtless)
he is a man who	he
in a hasty manner	hastily
this is a subject that	this subject
owing to the fact that	since [Avoid using *the fact that*.]

Politeness and service-mindedness are key elements in English business style. Thus, the use of polite phrases such as *We would appreciate it if, At your convenience, Please consider*, and *Thank you for your consideration* is considered good style. Note the service-mindedness reflected in the letter from Video Distributors (pages 132–133), in which David House emphasizes his interest in the success of Wilson Video.

Business writing style also strives for a fine balance between respect and equality between the persons who are communicating. The following examples will help you understand the proper balance.

1. Use *could, would,* or *might* to make what you write less blunt:

   That is impossible. [*blunt*]
   That would create unnecessary difficulties. [*more diplomatic*]

2. Do not present your ideas as an ultimatum.

   There is no possibility of meeting that deadline. [*ultimatum*]
   We find it difficult to meet the deadline. [*more diplomatic*]

3. Present your ideas more as opinion than as fact.

> Your figures are wrong. [*blunt*]
> We feel that your figures warrant revision. [*more diplomatic*]

4. Avoid using negative words.

> Your attitude is destructive. [*abrasive*]
> We would appreciate greater cooperation. [*more diplomatic*]

5. Present rejections as a result over which you had no control.

> I will not meet your salary demands. [*blunt*]
> I am afraid that our salary schedule does not allow us to meet your salary demands. [*more diplomatic*]

> *Note:* In rejecting demands, always preface your statement with a phrase like *I am (we are) sorry that* or *I am (we are) afraid that.*

6. Use the continuous form with words such as *think, hope, wonder,* and *plan.*

> I think you should accept our salary offer. [*blunt*]
> I was wondering whether you might accept our salary offer. [*more diplomatic*]

7. Do not adopt a subservient tone.

> We beg your forgiveness for our failure to meet the deadline. [*subservient*]
> Please excuse the delay in our delivery.

8. Try to elicit agreement.

> I think that you will agree that . . .

9. Use a question to make a proposal or express an opinion.

> Wouldn't it be better if . . .
> Don't you think this would be more appropriate?

10. Use qualifiers.

> We must express slight disagreement . . .
> We have some reservations . . .

11. In stating preference, use phrases like *We would rather* or *We prefer to.*

Exercises

Using Polite Phrases

Using the above or other polite phrases, rewrite the following sentences:

1. We cannot do that.
2. I don't want to meet you that early.
3. I want this by Thursday.

4. I cannot accept your proposal.
5. We expect you to accept an 8 percent commission.
6. That would create a problem.
7. Your analysis of the situation is incorrect.
8. Your claim for compensation has been rejected.
9. This year's sales results were bad.
10. We think it would be better if you changed your strategy.

Responding to a Complaint

Analyze the accompanying letter, explaining how the writer has managed to respond politely and diplomatically to a complaint concerning construction noise at a resort hotel.

Practicing Polite Responses

Write a letter using polite and diplomatic formulations in response to one of the following letters.

1. A letter of complaint due to delayed delivery of 100 Walkmans to an electronics store for which you are the major supplier.
2. A disagreement with the producer of tennis rackets for which you are the major distributor in your country. They have offered you a 7 percent commission on all sales, but you have requested 10 percent.
3. A letter from a dissatisfied tourist at one of your hotels complaining about construction noise. (Do not use the exact same wording as in the letter on page 142.)
4. Invent and describe a situation and then respond to it in the form of a letter.

Achieving an Active Style

Create an active style by focusing on verbs rather than nouns and by using the active voice.

Verb-Centered Writing

Note the emphasis on nouns that weakens the impact of this sentence:

> The committee made a *recommendation* that there was a *need* for an *improvement* in the company's billing routines.

This verb-centered approach is both more active and more concise:

> The committee *recommended* that the company *improve* its billing routines.

Active Versus Passive Voice

In the active voice, the reader sees immediately who did the action and what he/she did because the actor is in the subject's place in the sentence. In the passive voice, the reader must wait until the end of the sentence to see who did the

Dear Mr. Wyatt:

I was sorry to hear from your letter of 10 January that you were dissatisfied with your stay on Tenerife in December of last year.

I have just been in contact with our local represenative in Alcudia concerning the problems with the construction noise at the Hotel Playa del Sol. He confirmed that the hotel found it necessary to carry out the construction work during this period and that the decision had been made on very short notice.

Unfortunately, Mansfield Tours was not informed of the decision before your arrival at the hotel, which made it impossible for us to alter your accommodation arrangement before your departure from London. Those guests who contacted our representative at the hotel were offered the opportunity to stay at one of our five-star hotels in the neighboring town at no additional expense.

You have requested a 50 percent discount for the inconvenience caused by the construction work. Because the incident was brought to our attention after your arrival, and because other accommodations were in fact available to you, we are unfortunately not able to give such a substantial refund.

However, our company policy states that our customers should always be 100 percent satisfied with their holiday, and I would therefore like to offer you and your spouse a weekend trip to Amsterdam, including accommodations at the Plaza Hotel, at our expense.

On behalf of Mansfield Tours, I regret the inconvenience you experienced during your holiday, and I sincerely hope this offer is acceptable to you. The tickets will be issued to you as soon as you contact our office.

Should you have any questions, please do not hesitate to write or call us. We hope that we can be of service in connection with any of your future travel plans.

Yours sincerely,

David Smith
Customer Service Manager

action, and sometimes the actor is not mentioned at all. In general, the active voice is stronger.

> *Active voice:* The CEO made the decision.
>
> *Passive voice:* The decision was made by the CEO.

However, the passive voice can be used when you wish to say what was done without pointing the finger at anyone. The passive voice allows you to be more diplomatic by allowing you to make your point without embarrassing anyone.

> *Example:* An excellent opportunity to penetrate the Canadian market was lost.

AN AUDIENCE-CENTERED APPROACH TO WRITING

Remember that you are communicating your ideas to an audience. In order to be effective, you *must* consider your audience's situation and priorities. When communicating, think of carrying on a dialogue with your audience. After you have written a couple of sentences, ask yourself what your audience would say to you after reading those sentences. Their interpretation of these preliminary sentences will influence how they interpret the remainder of your communication. Their response will be *cumulative* — that is, each sentence they read will influence how they interpret the rest of the communication.

The goal of much of your communication will be to get your audience to act in a specific way. To achieve this goal, you must formulate your communication in a way that is attractive to your audience. Thus, you must balance your goal of persuading the audience to act in a certain way with a consideration of their priorities and needs. Thus, you should provide them with the information they need and show how acting in the desired fashion *will benefit them*. For example, say your boss is under pressure to cut production costs and has asked you to evaluate production routines. You have researched the subject and developed routines that will cut costs in the long run, but will result in high initial costs. In order to persuade your boss, you must think of her situation:

1. She is under pressure due to the high costs of production.
2. She is of the old school of labor-intensive assembly.
3. She is very concerned with quality control.
4. Her boss is a "number cruncher" (a person who is concerned about costs).

Thus, your report cannot simply provide a conclusion to convert to robot-centered production. You must appeal to your boss's quality-control priority in order to overcome her reluctance to convert from a labor-intensive approach to a robot-centered approach. You can show that factory X, your competitor which uses the same robot-centered production system, has a record of only 2 percent of finished products that do not meet quality standards. Furthermore, you must also provide her with figures that will (a) convince her number-crunching boss that the initial investment will be profitable and (b) predict when this new system will pay back the initial investment. You must provide your boss with enough "ammunition" to look good when confronting her own boss. If she looks good, you look good, and your idea will be accepted. You might even be promoted to manage the conversion.

The main thing is not to assume that your audience automatically thinks as you do. Analyze their situation and priorities and appeal to them. Remember that communication is a dialogue, not a monologue.

Appendix 3
ELECTRONIC
COMMUNICATION
DEVICES

In our age of electronic communication, a few words must be said about such communication devices.

E-MAIL

Electronic mail, or E-Mail, is second only to FAX messages in speed of transmission. Whereas a letter to Europe from the United States may take seven to nine days, an E-Mail letter takes less than thirty minutes. Your letter is electronically transmitted via your computer, which must be connected either to a modem or directly to a mainframe computer. It allows you to transmit messages to anyone who has a similar set-up and an E-Mail address. This address consists of a user identification code (ID) + @ + the computer network address, also known as the *node name*. The fee for a user code is nominal, and the cost of transmission usually depends on your position. Most university faculty can send E-Mail free, for example, while most students are on a pay-as-you-go basis.

When using E-Mail in a business setting, remember that initial contacts should be established by formal business letters. Once a working relationship is established, however, E-Mail can be an efficient means of communication.

ELECTRONIC BULLETIN BOARDS

Electronic bulletin boards are open forums accessed through your computer. Let us say that you are an Apple user and want to access other Apple users to share experience and ask questions. You can access a bulletin board called AppleLink directly or through *Internet* (a worldwide network of interconnected computers to exchange information) by typing in the access code for AppleLink. Either way you must have an account number, which you get by paying a nominal fee to either Internet or AppleLink. Once you are into the bulletin board, you can type your message or question, which will show up on your screen and that of any other screen logged on to this AppleLink. Other users can then respond to your message or question, and their responses will appear on all screens logged on to AppleLink. There are many such bulletin boards which provide access to a great deal of expertise. You should become aware of electronic bulletin boards in your field of interest.

INDEX

About the Author

DREW RODGERS teaches business communication and English at the Norwegian School of Management. His twenty-seven years of teaching experience at colleges and universities in the United States, Switzerland, and Norway include courses in business communication, British and American studies, writing, and literature.

Instructor's Manual to Accompany

Business Communications

INTERNATIONAL CASE STUDIES
IN ENGLISH

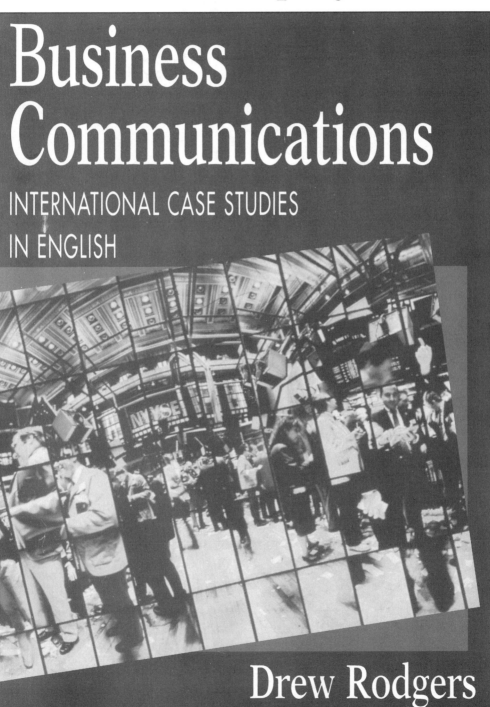

Drew Rodgers

Manufactured in the United States of America.

9 8 7 6 5
f e d c b a

For information, write:
St. Martin's Press, Inc.
175 Fifth Avenue
New York, NY 10010

ISBN 0-312-11172-x

Contents

WELCOME

Welcome to <u>Business Communications</u>, a multipurpose book that allows you, the teacher, to select from a variety of resources and tailor their uses to your specific class situation. The case study method develops both oral and written English as well as teamwork, problem solving, information gathering, and presentation skills. Thus, students appreciate the methodology underlying the case study approach because they know that they need these skills in any business situation. The use of both closed and open-ended cases (described in more detail below) is, to my knowledge, unique in books of this sort. The closed-ended cases are at the beginning of the book and supply all the necessary information to solve the cases, with the exception of Case 1, "Job Search: Preparing for Your Future," for which students must research a local company. The open-ended cases are set in the students' local environment and require them to obtain information from that environment. Thus, they are realistic and build on the skills developed in the closed-ended cases.

The case study method will actively engage your students and thus provide them an optimal opportunity to learn both language and communication skills. Its use has been widely acclaimed and, judging from my students, this acclaim is well justified.

AUDIENCE

<u>Business Communications</u> is intended for advanced-intermediate to advanced students who are preparing to be or presently are business majors, as well as for business people who wish to improve their English and communication skills. The cases allow for the development of both oral and written skills, and written assignments are suggested for each case. In addition, a section on business writing is included to aid in teaching written skills.

A business background is <u>not</u> a requirement for this course, as students are encouraged to share their knowledge to help create the atmosphere of cooperation fundamental to the case study approach. Those cases that require the least amount of business background are:

Job Search: Preparing for Your Future (Case 1)
Marketing Negotiations: Long-range Golf Equipment Seeks a Distributor
(Case 4)
Labor Relations: Midland Heating and Cooling vs. the Primary Sheet Metal
Workers of America, AFL-CIO (Case 5)
Environment and Business Leaders' Social Responsibility: Northern Electrical
Services vs. the Environmentalists (Case 6)
Business Organization and Management: Commutair: Employee Motivation
and Management Theory (Case 7)
Business Organization and Management: Unhealthy Leaders: Sterling Forklift
(Case 8)

1

APPROACH

The Case Study Method and Its Application

The case study method is based on the approach used in M.B.A. programs at Harvard Business School and at many other major schools of business. It has been adapted to teach ESP both in Europe and in inventive programs in the United States. It is better adapted to teaching ESP-Business than the traditional teacher-centered approach because it develops communicative competence by putting the students in the center of the action where they can use language actively and practice communication skills. Think about the traditional teacher-centered method in which the teacher is the hub and all communication goes through him or her. Learning a language and communication skills requires active participation and if only one student can speak at a time, how much learning can be accomplished? With the case study method, on the other hand, students are allowed to interact in their individual groups, thus multiplying the opportunity to produce language and to receive feedback, as well as to practice communication skills.

This method does not exclude teacher-centered segments. They are integrated when defining and clarifying the cases or working on grammar and vocabulary. However, once such segments are completed, students should be allowed to interact not only to learn English in the most efficient and enjoyable manner, but also to learn communication, teamwork, problem solving, presentation, and networking skills.

The Teacher's Role

For those who have not used the case study method and thus are a bit insecure in its use, rest assured that it is one of the easiest methods once the proper mindset has been adopted. In this method, the teacher functions as a facilitator in engaging the students and a resource person in providing vocabulary and language feedback. It is important to create the proper mood. Thus, the first class hours are extremely important. Two areas of expertise should be defined, the teacher's being language and the students' being a knowledge of business subjects. Show respect for student knowledge and encourage its use. This will establish an equality in the relationship between teacher and students that will encourage students' participation. Naturally the teacher will learn a great deal about business, too, which will be helpful in future teaching. One cannot teach this course and not learn--another advantage with this method.

The teacher's role consists of:

1. <u>Insuring that the cases and students' individual roles in solving them are clearly understood.</u> Students must have a clear idea of their individual roles. Otherwise they can get frustrated. Even worse, they may misconstrue their roles. Thus, after clearly presenting the case (explained under "Teaching Sequence" below) and its objectives and having the students repeat their roles to make sure they understand them, let them start preparing their roles in class. This serves four purposes: (1) you can answer any questions the students might have about the case; (2) you can help them get started; (3) you can "cross-fertilize" (for example, in overhearing one group's preparation in a negotiations case, you can go to the opponents' group preparing on the other side of the room and ask, "What would you do if your opponents proposed an 8 percent commission on all sales?"); and (4) you can insure that students speak English all the time. If you have time in class, you should use it for part of the case preparation as you then insure that everything is done in English. A fifty-fifty approach, in which students are expected to use an hour or so outside class for every hour in class for case preparation seems reasonable.

2. <u>Being a benevolent police officer.</u> You enforce the basic rules of the course that you establish during the first class hour: (1) use English (remind students that English is the <u>lingua franca</u> of the course and is the only language to be used in class), and (2) be active (everyone in the group must participate).

3. <u>Acting as a resource person.</u> Go around from group to group during the case preparation and provide any vocabulary the students need.

4. <u>Providing feedback.</u> At the end of the preparation and presentation periods, give both language and content feedback noted during these phases. This can be done on the board by writing vocabulary words that the students lacked and you supplied. Similarly, mistakes in grammar can be corrected, either by writing sentences containing (1) the actual mistakes or (b) blanks at the points where the mistakes appeared, and having students correct the sentences.

5. <u>Teaching communication skills.</u> You will find that you are teaching a whole range of skills, as mentioned above, and one of these is presentation technique. In the beginning of the semester, you should teach the students steps in making a good presentation, including (a) choosing and limiting the topic, (b) researching it, (c) organizing it, and (d) presenting it (through the use of audio-visual techniques, body language, audience-grabbing techniques, and so on).

Those of you who have used the case study method know how well it works. Those of you who haven't are in for an enjoyable teaching experience. Good luck.

COURSE INTRODUCTION The course introduction, which takes the first two hours of the course, is vitally important in establishing the proper atmosphere. In this introduction, you should emphasize several points. First and foremost, state that twenty-one (given twenty students and one teacher) heads are better than one. The point is that the students are just as important as the teacher and that the course is student-oriented. Second, stress that the students are business experts and will be expected to share their knowledge with each other. Third, emphasize the importance of networking (developing of contacts and the sharing of knowledge). Underline this by noting that if we could collectively share all the knowledge we possessed, we would be "dynamite." The intention is to create an atmosphere of cooperation and an active orientation toward the material. By stressing that the students are the business experts, you boost their confidence so that they will be encouraged to participate actively in each case.

      Establish the three basic rules of the class:

1. Speak only English in class, except when asking how to say something in English.
2. Be active.
3. Be prepared to play assigned roles on the day the case will be presented.

      Introduce the case study method and the sequencing presented below and discuss students' roles, including reading the cases in advance of their introduction, formulating opinions regarding the discussion questions, preparing the roles in the cases, and learning the vocabulary.

      Promote the class (it never hurts to market your product) by informing students of the skills they will develop (in addition to language skills) and stressing how important these skills are in the business world:

1. How to make public presentations.
2. How to network and increase one's knowledge of the business world.
3. How to work in teams.
4. How to find necessary information.
5. How to deal with foreign cultures and their values and ways of doing business.
6. How to solve problems.

GROUP FORMATION After introducing the course, help the students form groups. The groups are extremely important as they will form the basis of the course work (given that roles will be assigned to groups). One way is to have the students pretend that they are at a cocktail party. You can even have them bring drinks and snacks to create a realistic atmosphere. At the "party" they can go around and introduce themselves to each other and talk in order to select the people with whom they would like to work in a group. Once that is completed, they are ready to work. Having students choose their own group members works for two reasons: (1) they will choose people with whom they can work well, and (2) they will get used to being active. While the "cocktail party" is going on note language mistakes, and after the "party" go over the mistakes on the board. This establishes the class's basic pattern of performance and feedback.

TEACHING SEQUENCE FOR THE INDIVIDUAL CASES The following sequence is applicable to most of the cases.

First hour: The students are assigned to read the case in advance and be prepared to make a case introduction in which they explain the case, the background and problem involved, and the students' roles. The teacher supplements what the students omit to insure that they have a complete understanding of the case. Roles are either determined by the students on a first-come-first-serve basis or assigned by the teacher. *It is important that the individual roles and goals of the case are clearly understood.* For example, in Case 4 ("Long-range Golf Equipment Seeks a Distributor") you want to establish that you have two negotiating teams, one representing a golf club manufacturer and the other representing a potential distributor, who are going to negotiate a contract involving the questions of an exclusive versus nonexclusive agreement, the rate of commission, and so on. The goal is to reach a contract acceptable to both parties.

Discussion of the discussion questions provided in each case. There are two sets of questions, one in the students' book and one in the Instructor's Manual. The former are to be used to establish the proper framework of thinking for the case. The latter require some business experience to answer and can be used to replace or supplement the questions in the students' book, especially with students who have business experience. In addition, the cultural background sections provide an excellent basis for the discussion of cultural differences, which will help the students understand their own culture as well as the cultural setting of the case.

Second hour: Class preparation of the group or individual roles. This will give you the opportunity to (1) make sure that the students have understood their roles and the goal of the case, (2) help the students get started if they have any problems, (3) "cross-fertilize," or share information from one group to another (for example, in the "Long-range Seeks a Distributor" case you might overhear that Long-range is only willing to offer a 6 percent commission; you can go to a second group and ask, "What if Long-range is only willing to offer 6 percent? What will your counteroffer be?"), and (4) note mistakes and vocabulary to take up at the end of this hour.

This hour can also be used for work in pairs, in order to practice the Language Mastery Exercises, which should be assigned as homework.

It is preferable to complete the first two phases in one sitting so that students have a clear picture of their roles before leaving class. Thus, two-hour blocks are recommended. If you have one-hour blocks, ask the groups to discuss outside of class what roles they wish to play and what those roles involve as preparation for the second meeting. As homework after the second meeting, students will be expected to prepare their roles either as a group or as individuals depending on the case and how they divide the role-play preparation, as well as to practice the vocabulary in sentences in pairs. Students will be expected, if possible, to spend time outside of class preparing for the case presentation. If this is not possible, one more class hour should be provided for preparation of the presentation.

Third hour: The case presentation (dramatization of the case). Your role is to note grammar and vocabulary mistakes to be reviewed in the next hour along with comments about content.

Fourth hour: Feedback on content, language (correction of mistakes made during the presentation), and vocabulary. In terms of content, you can consider how effective their negotiating strategy was, how impressive the interview was, how convincing their arguments were, or how they functioned in a group presentation, depending on the case.

Most of the cases fit into this time frame. However, some cases, such as "Preparing for Your Future" (Case 1), "Competing Internationally" (Case 13), and "Saturn" (Case 14) may take longer. A suggested step-by-step teaching sequence is provided for each case below.

<u>Language Elements and Assignments</u>

TEACHING VOCABULARY One of the primary aims of this book is to teach vocabulary, as it is one of the areas in which most students are weak. Thus, the cases come complete with vocabulary lists. The question is how the students can best acquire vocabulary. Your job is to make learning vocabulary interesting (a task that is aided by the case study method and the inherent opportunity to use words in context). Thus, you want to encourage your students to use as many of the words in their presentations as possible. There are various ways of doing this. First, encourage the students to use as many of the vocabulary words in the book as possible in the case preparation and presentation. Second, if you grade their presentations, part of the grade can be based on vocabulary. Third, you can begin each session with a quick vocabulary drill in which you randomly select students and have them define a given word from the book and use it in a sentence that brings out its meaning. Fourth, you can have periodic written vocabulary quizzes that require students to use words in sentences that illustrate their meanings. Fifth, in listening to students' preparation and presentations, correct misused vocabulary. As part of the feedback session after the preparation and presentations, go over vocabulary, (either words that were misused, or words that students lacked and that had to be supplied). Write them on the board as an assignment for next time, when students will be asked to use them in sentences.

TEACHING GRAMMAR Students are reluctant to study grammar as an end in itself. However, that does not mean that grammar should not be taught; it is simply a question of method. Grammar should be taught as a part of the post-preparation and post-presentation stages. While the students are doing their in-class preparation and the case presentation, you should note the mistakes that they make. As part of the feedback session, go over grammar mistakes by putting the incorrect sentences on the board and having students correct them. Ask students to make correct sentences with the grammatical construction in question and ask them to explain *why* they use the particular grammatical construction. An understanding of *why* is as important as using the correct grammatical form. The students will be much more responsive to this approach, as they will have visible proof on the board that they have not yet mastered the grammatical construction in question.

ASSIGNMENTS The number of assignments will depend on your students. If your class consists of business people, the amount of time they have outside class will be limited. They should concentrate primarily on reading the cases in advance of class and preparing their roles for the case solution and presentation, learning the vocabulary in sentences, and studying and practicing the Language Mastery exercises. Every student should have read the case before the day it is introduced. In fact, the students should introduce the case by telling what it involves--describing the various roles to be played and the case's goals. They should have also thought about answers to the discussion questions. If your students are full-time students, you might wish to add other exercises at your discretion.

A business writing section is provided in the book to help complete the written assignments. The number of written assignments is left to your discretion, depending on the focus of your course and the needs of your students. The cases generate the information necessary to complete the written assignments and thus motivate the students to write more than would be the case if a writing assignment were given without the preliminary case preparation.

BIBLIOGRAPHIC REFERENCES AND VIDEOS The cases come complete with references to support materials to help the students solve them. Most of the cases can be solved without support material. However, based on the level of your students and the cases chosen, determine what support material is needed and make sure that it is available.

THE CASES

CASE 1/Job Search: Preparing for Your Future

There is a logic in the order in which the cases are presented in this book. Case 1, "Job Search: Preparing for Your Future," helps to break the ice as well as to reinforce the teaching philosophy behind this course. This case should effectively create the atmosphere for the rest of the semester. The case should be preceded by the introduction of the course as described above in order to establish the course's basic student-centered philosophy. Case 1 helps reinforce this as its focus is on the students. First, it allows each student to get to know the members of his or her group. Second, it gets the students talking about themselves; it is easier to get students talking about themselves than any other subject. Third, it demonstrates that the teacher is interested in the students' future. Fourth, it shows that the cases have a connection with the real world. Fifth, it forces the students to find information outside the classroom, a skill which will be useful in later open-ended cases such as Cases 10, 13, and 14.

Good support in presenting this case can often be provided by the Career Services office if one is available at your school. Counselors are often willing to give a seminar on résumé and cover letter writing, as well as tips concerning the job search and interviewing.

A good way to begin this case is to ask students what they have done to start planning their careers and to find jobs. This will introduce them to networking, in which they share their ideas and strategies to improve their chances of finding a job. What you are doing is helping them to work out a job-finding strategy. Another good discussion is about dos and don'ts in résumé and cover letter writing. Here, you can consult a business communications textbook or contact Career Services. Finally, discuss dos and don'ts in an interview. Naturally, you will first ask the students for their input and then fill in if necessary.

CASE GOALS

1. To set the student-centered tone of the class discussed above.
2. To break the ice and allow the students to get to know each other.
3. To develop a team spirit and get the group members used to delegating responsibility and reporting findings to the group.
4. To practice individual presentations in an interview context.
5. To practice letter and résumé writing with an emphasis on format and proper business tone.

CLASS SESSIONS

First hour: Either (a) an introduction about résumé and cover letter writing by a counselor from Career Services, or (b) a discussion of what the students have done to start planning their careers plus the discussion questions in the student book. Language feedback.

Be sure to tell students about the plans for the second hour in advance, asking them to bring newspapers or professional journals or to cut out advertisements so that they are ready to select the company and job. (Note: Take some copies of relevant job advertisements and have them available in case some students do not bring newspapers or journals.)

Second hour: Group work in which each group chooses the company to which they will be applying; they either find an advertisement for a job in a newspaper or write an advertisement geared to their interests and background. If the advertisement is in a foreign language, it must be translated into English. If the group members have different backgrounds, they may need several jobs, in which case they may have to create the jobs and the advertisements. However, the jobs should be in the same company so that they do not have to research several companies. Remember, the group members will be both candidates and selection team members and thus will have to know about the company that they have selected. The groups should assign the various tasks associated with the case to various group members as homework (for example, getting information about the company, finishing the advertisements, and so on). Language feedback.

Third hour: Have each group discuss the material about the company that the assigned group member(s) found out, including what activities the company is involved in, what they are looking for in a candidate, and other information that can come from annual reports and informational interviews with the Human Resources department of the company to which they are "applying." Language feedback.

Fourth hour: A writing seminar in which the students write résumés and letters of application individually while the teacher helps with language. Career Services may be helpful in this exercise. This can be optional depending on how much help the students need. The résumé and letter of application assignment can be done as homework to be handed in. But the résumés and letters of application must be circulated to the other group members before the interview so as to give them adequate time to develop questions for each candidate. In any case, the students should provide one copy of their résumé and letter of application to each group member and to the teacher for correction.

OR, a second possibility is a practice interview using the general questions in the student book. Language feedback.

Fifth hour: If the fourth session was devoted to a writing seminar, then use this session to practice answering interview questions. Otherwise, this session will be devoted to the "real" interviews of about ten minutes each.

Sixth hour: "Real" interviews of about seven minutes each for classes with the writing seminar. This allows enough time at the end of class for each group to present to the class as a whole the candidate who received the job and to explain why. Classes that did not have the writing seminar can take more time for the presentation of the candidate selected and the explanation why--as well as those candidates who were not selected and why not. Language and content feedback from the fifth and sixth hours.

This case is more difficult to schedule than the others, so you must use your own discretion, in accordance with the level of the students and the availability of a Career Services office.

WORK EXPERIENCE: QUESTIONS FOR STUDENTS   Discuss an interview situation that you have had. What questions were you asked? What did you do that was successful? What mistakes did you make? What tips can you give to help others prepare for and present themselves in an interview?   This information can be shared in the third session.

CASE 2/Investment: Portfolio Development

The goals of this case are clearly set out in the "Case" section. Students will present their findings to the class and explain why they chose the investments they did. They will have to defend their choices, and the other students in the class should be encouraged to critically evaluate the presenters' choices. A healthy argument is always stimulating.

It is only fair to give the students chosen to present a day or two to prepare their presentation, especially as they are going to need to use visual aids. In this case, you advance students' presentation skills by requiring them to be convincing and to support their decision through the use of visual aids and figures. In addition, they get some practice in presenting under pressure.

This case could form the basis of a contest with the best portfolio at the end of the semester being the winner. Students often like competition, and the effect could be heightened by a prize provided by the school or the teacher. Vocabulary is an integral part of this case and the preparation and presentation will require using many of the words on the list. Thus, it is not necessary to drill vocabulary.

CASE GOALS

1.   To teach students presentation skills, including the use of visual aids and the structuring of a presentation into introduction, body, and conclusion. The introduction should include
     (a) a brief statement of the subject and a division into subtopics which

10

can be presented via an overhead projector;

(b) a "hook" to get the audience interested in the topic, such as a statement along the lines of "My portfolio's value will increase by an estimated 30 percent this year and the tips I give you can be worth their weight in gold"; and

(c) a brief statement of the presenter's expertise to add weight to the value of his or her presentation.

The body will include the analysis of various investment possibilities and an explanation of why the student has chosen his or her investments. It is important that the students learn to support their claims, and the use of data displayed on overheads is an important part of this case. The conclusion will briefly summarize the portfolio, why it was chosen, and what growth potential it has. (See the worksheet for students below.)

2.　　To teach the vocabulary of investment.

PRESENTATION WORKSHEET

Introduction

1.　　What am I going to talk about (the topic)?
2.　　How is the presentation going to be divided? Subtopics might include (a) investment goals and strategies, (b) the instruments in general (stocks, metals, bonds, and so on), (c) specific investments (which stocks, bonds, and the like), and why they are good investments, (d) expected trends in the market, and so on.
3.　　Why should you the audience listen to me--what can you expect to learn and how can you profit by listening to me?
4.　　My expertise--what experience do I have that qualifies me to speak on this subject?

Body Subtopics such as those as presented in number 2 above.

Conclusion A summary of your portfolio, expected growth in its value, and why you expect this growth.

CLASS SESSIONS

First hour: As homework in preparation for this case, have the students study the vocabulary and bring a copy of the financial section of the local or national newspaper.

Have a discussion of the various types of investments. This can be limited to stocks, allowing the portfolios to be based on stocks alone. Get the students to share their knowledge. This case provides opportunities for

11

students to teach each other. If your students are not capable of that, try to get someone from another department, perhaps a teaching assistant or lecturer, to come in or use the video mentioned below (under "Necessary Background Information"). Discuss the discussion questions. If these are too difficult, have students express opinions about investing. Would they invest money at all, and if so in what investments and why? Try to get them to defend their opinions. Have the students choose partners (probably someone from their own group). Homework for the second session is to be able to discuss the rise and fall of the share prices for companies represented on the graphs using the vocabulary provided in the book. You can also bring graphs on transparencies and ask the students to describe the rise and fall of, for example, the Dow Jones Index, oil prices, or other stocks over time. Language feedback.

Second hour: The exercise describing the rise and fall of stocks, indexes, oil prices, etc. The pairs work out their portfolios. Language feedback.

Third hour: Some of the pairs present their portfolios.

Fourth hour: Language and content feedback from the third and fourth hours.

NECESSARY BACKGROUND INFORMATION This is a complicated area, but the Wall Street Journal video on "Money and Markets" or a lecture on investment can provide a basic introduction that should be adequate to help the students solve the case.

WORK EXPERIENCE: QUESTIONS FOR STUDENTS What current investments would you recommend and why? What is the best investment you ever made?

CASE 3/Other People's Money: Larry the Liquidator vs. New England Wire and Cable

The purpose of this case is to continue the presentation and training of the previous case while introducing argumentation. Both the management team and Larry Garfinkle's team will have to present their cases to the stockholders based on the figures from the annual report and prognoses for the coming year, as well as any other arguments that they choose to use. In addition, the stockholders chosen to defend their vote will have to justify their position.

This case also has a consciousness-raising function in making the students aware of what is going on in terms of M & A (mergers and acquisitions), which is a major force shaping the corporate picture today. The recommended articles provide a balanced picture that serves as a basis for the discussion questions. Too often, business majors are not forced to confront the social or environmental consequences of their decisions. Thus, cases that take up these questions are included in this book.

This case could provide an opportunity for a social evening based on a showing of the video of *Other People's Money*. A social evening helps unify a class, and the third week is a strategically sound time to have it. By then, the students know each other well enough to feel secure and yet benefit from getting to know each other better. Buy a copy of the video in case it goes out of production. After viewing the video, you can have one of the discussions mentioned in the case and/or have some social activities.

CASE GOALS

1. Consciousness-raising to help students consider the social consequences of business decisions.
2. The development of argumentation skills. Too often students simply state their point of view but do not support it with facts and logic. The worksheets below should help them develop better argumentation skills. To fill out the first worksheet, students should write a statement and then find figures or logic to support the statement. For the counterargumentation worksheet, they should anticipate three of their opponent's points and then find counterarguments and support for these counterarguments.
3. Learning meeting terminology.

ARGUMENTATION EXERCISE WORKSHEET Find three arguments for your point of view and then support them with facts or logic.

<u>Example</u> *Statement (Garfinkle):* If you accept my offer, you will realize a quick profit.

Support: My offer is 15 percent above the present market price of the stock.

COUNTERARGUMENTATION EXERCISE WORKSHEET Anticipate three arguments your opponents might use and then find counterarguments and support.

<u>Example</u> *Anticipated argument (Jorgensen):* Garfinkle has offered you an immediate 15 percent profit based on the present market value of New England Wire and Cable stock.

Counterargument: If you wait one year, you will be able to realize an even greater profit.

Support: New England Wire and Cable stock is presently undervalued and that is why Garfinkle is interested in it. With the building of bridges and highways that the U.S. government is going to undertake, we estimate an increase in profits reaching $1 million already next year, which means that our dividend and stock price will increase significantly. Why take l5 percent now when you very well might make a 25 to 33 percent profit in a year?

CLASS SESSIONS

First hour: Discuss the movie or play and the discussion questions. Assign roles, including: Jorgensen's team and Garfinkle's team, with the rest of the class acting as stockholders with a specific number of shares which they can vote. The easiest would be to give them all 100 shares so the vote will be equal. Language feedback.

Second hour: Begin with a quick review of meeting terminology. Ask questions such as "What do you say to open the meeting, to make a proposal," and so on. Then the two teams should prepare their presentations while the stockholders discuss their feelings about the upcoming meeting, including the pros and cons of the takeover bid. Language feedback.

Third hour: The meeting. If there is time after the meeting the stockholders should get together in their groups and discuss their views. Which side do they support and why?

Fourth hour: The vote should be taken and some students asked to state and justify their position. Language and content feedback from the third and fouth hours.

NECESSARY BACKGROUND INFORMATION Showing the video or reading the play *Other People's Money* by Jerry Sterner should provide enough information to solve the case. The article "Simplicity Pattern" in Donald Bartlett and James Steele's America: What Went Wrong (Kansas City: Andrews and McMeel, 1992) will provide enough fuel for an interesting discussion for advanced students with business experience. The case can be solved without an in-depth knowledge of corporate raiding, so you must decide how in-depth the case should be. A more involved analysis can be provided by a guest lecturer, perhaps a business professor or graduate student.

WORK EXPERIENCE: QUESTIONS FOR STUDENTS Has a company for which you have worked been the target of a hostile takeover or merger? What impact did that have on the atmosphere and the morale at the company? Did the management do anything to help lessen the negative impact of the takeover or merger? What happened to the company in terms of layoffs, stripping, etc., as a result of the takeover or merger?

CASE 4/Marketing Negotiations: Long-range Golf Equipment Seeks a Distributor

In this case we get into negotiations. We cross the line from purely teaching ESP to teaching content in that we take up the question of negotiation theory. The information in the case provides the basis, but you can bring your own knowledge of negotiations to bear on a class discussion. The students could discuss a theoretical situation where a couple has a dilemma. One person wants to stay home and watch television and the other wants to go to the cinema. Ask how the students would tackle the problem and how they would negotiate a solution. Then analyze their approach. Use this to start a debate on negotiation theory and tactics. See what they know about negotiating and how they would approach the above negotiation. Discuss the importance of arriving at a mutually satisfying contract in establishing a continuing relationship like the one between supplier and distributor. What tone would the students expect in such negotiations?

Emphasize the importance of having a clear strategy before entering negotiations and have all the teams fill out a negotiations worksheet (provided in the case), which they are to hand in.

In this case it is important to "cross-fertilize." This means listening to both sides' preparation, then going back and forth and asking, "What would you do if the other side proposed X or Y?" In this way, you are preparing both sides for the negotiations, insuring that they run more smoothly and efficiently.

The following information should be given to the XYZ negotiating team:

Year	Brand / Sales		Commission	Income
1992	Tiger Shark	$3,000,000	7%	$ 210,000
	Hurricane	2,500,000	7%	175,000
1993	Tiger Shark	5,000,000	7%	350,000
	Hurricane	4,000,000	7%	280,000
1994	Tiger Shark	6,000,000	7%	420,000
	Hurricane	5,000,000	7%	350,000

This information is necessary in determining whether to go along with an exclusive contract, as XYZ would be gambling the loss of the income generated by the sales of Tiger Shark and Hurricane equipment. Because Long-range clubs are untested in the market, I would recommend to the XYZ team that they reject the exclusive contract offer of Long-range for at least a two-year period, to give XYZ an opportunity to evaluate the equipment's market performance. After the two-year period, the contract could be renegotiated and the question of an exclusive contract could be reconsidered. XYZ should also demand that Long-range mount and pay for a nationwide promotion.

The following information should be given to the Long-range negotiating team: Your marketing department has investigated XYZ and determined that they are a reputable company that specializes in sporting gear for the mid- to upper-price range market. They do not carry major brands such as Ping, but have been very successful with Tiger Shark and Hurricane. They completed a successful launch of these two brands and in two years have captured 5 percent of the total market. Furthermore, distributors who carry major brands would probably not carry Long-range, and if they did, would never consider an exclusive contract. Long-range golf equipment would have a very low priority with major distributors. Your marketing department recommends XYZ as the best possibility to penetrate the mid- to upper-price range market throughout Great Britain. One other possibility would be British Golf Imports, which distributes imported golf equipment. However, they have not been as successful as XYZ and already distribute four brands of golf equipment that have captured only 3 percent of the British market after five years. They would probably accept a new brand, but it would be placed alongside the other brands.

If you discover during the preparation phase that the two sides are far apart in terms of the commission, you might suggest a sliding scale, for example 6 percent on the first $1 million, 7 percent on the next $1 million, and so on, to help achieve a compromise.

CASE GOALS

1.   Develop an awareness of cultural differences and their impact on negotiations.
2.   Develop language and strategic skills for negotiations.

CLASS SESSIONS

First hour: The discussion about negotiation strategy based on information given in the case. An interesting discussion can be based on a comparison of negotiation styles within the students' country or countries and that illustrated in this case about American negotiation style and traits. Assignment of roles. Students should discuss the discussion questions separately in groups, as these will form the basis of their negotiation strategy. Language feedback.

Second hour: The teams should fill out the negotiation worksheet and prepare their strategy for the negotiation. Language feedback.

Third hour: The negotiation.

Fourth hour: Presentation of the results of the negotiation. XYZ and Long-range present together, stating the conditions of the final contract. Each side should present its strategy, its goals, and an analysis of its success in achieving these goals. Language and content feedback for the third and fourth hours.

NECESSARY BACKGROUND INFORMATION As mentioned above, a discussion of the approaches to negotiation within various cultures would be an interesting introduction to this case, especially given the global-market nature of the world's economy. Dynamics of Successful International Business Negotiations by Moran and Stripp (Gulf Publishing Co., 1991) or similar books can provide valuable insights to help fuel the discussion.

WORK EXPERIENCE: QUESTIONS FOR STUDENTS Have you recently been involved in any kind of negotiation situation? Describe the situation, your preparation and strategy, the actual negotiation, and the result. How successful was your strategy? Why did it succeed or fail? What cultural differences, if any, did you experience?

CASE 5/Labor Relations: Midland Heating and Cooling vs. The Primary Sheet Metal Workers of America, AFL-CIO

This is a follow-up case to Long-range in which students can hone their negotiating skills in English. Refer to the preceding Long-range case to see how to introduce the idea of negotiating. Because this is a union versus management case, the tone of the negotiations will probably be harsher. However, you should ask the class to discuss how the negotiations will differ from those in the Long-range case just to get their input. It is important in this case that the students understand what is being negotiated. Go through all points to be sure that the students understand them. For example, the union's demands:

- No subcontracting means that a portion of the production cannot be done by subcontractors as this takes work away from Midland and increases the possibility of layoffs.

- No part-time work is important, as part-time workers do not enjoy certain benefits like health insurance. An employer can cut expenses by hiring part-time workers.

- A no-layoff guarantee is important in a time when manufacturing companies are laying off large numbers of employees, often moving production to cheaper areas such as the southern United States and Mexico.

- COLAs (cost of living adjustments) are a common union demand to counteract the effect of inflation. (However, management rarely concedes this demand.)

- Job posting--requiring all jobs to be announced through the union.

You should go through all the demands and have the students explain what they are and their importance to each side.

CASE GOALS To further develop the skills emphasized in "Long-range Golf Equipment Seeks a Distributor."

CLASS SESSIONS Follow the same pattern as in "Long-range Golf Equipment Seeks a Distributor." During the second meeting, review common negotiation phrases by asking questions such as "What would you say to make sure that you have understood, to express a willingness to cooperate," and so on.

NECESSARY BACKGROUND INFORMATION The information provided here and in the student text should be adequate to solve this case.

WORK EXPERIENCE: QUESTIONS FOR STUDENTS Have you recently been involved in a wage negotiation situation? Describe the situation, your preparation and strategy, the actual negotiation and the result. How successful was your strategy? Why did it succeed or fail?

POSITION PAPERS To be handed out to the respective teams.

Union Negotiation Position The union surveyed the employees' preferences and the poll showed the following results:

Economic Item	% Listed	% Listed No. 1
Wage increase	93	60
COLAs (Cost of Living Adjustments)	89	15
Fully paid health insurance	81	14
Life insurance	64	7
Additional paid vacation leave	59	4

Noneconomic Item	% Listed	% Listed No. 1
A no-layoff guarantee	99	97
No subcontracting	91	1
No part-time employment	89	1
Job-posting program	84	

This will form the basis of your negotiation strategy. Although a wage increase, cost of living adjustment, and fully paid health insurance dominate the workers' economic demands, they must be weighed against the job security issues that dominate the noneconomic demands. Prepare a negotiation worksheet (see "Long-range Golf Equipment Seeks a Distributor" for the worksheet and information on negotiation strategy) in which you establish your "musts" (high priority demands that you must get), medium-priority demands, and trading cards (low-priority demands that you are willing to trade away for concessions from management). In terms of your trading cards, establish what concessions from management you expect in return for your concessions. Remember, you have to go back to the workers with the contract for their approval; thus you must acknowledge the demands expressed in the above poll.

Management Negotiation Position You are faced with increasing competition and falling sales and market shares, and naturally you want to cut costs. However, you know that the union representatives will point to increased productivity and a 2 percent drop in members' buying power over the contract's last three-year period. You also know that job security is a primary concern. So you might consider developing a strategy in which you emphasize the union's probable noneconomic demands, such as a no-layoff guarantee, no subcontracting, no part-time employment, and job posting. You definitely don't want to go above a 4 percent pay raise per year and are strongly against a cost of living adjustment (COLA), as it makes cost estimation of future contracts difficult. Prepare a negotiation worksheet that forms the basis of your negotiation strategy (see "Long-range Golf Equipment Seeks a Distributor" for the worksheet and information on negotiation strategy). You must establish your "musts" (high-priority demands that you must get), your medium-priority demands, and your "trading cards" (low-priority demands that you are willing to trade away for concessions from the union). In terms of your trading cards, establish what concessions from the union you expect in return for your concessions.

CASE 6/Environment and Business Leaders' Social Responsibility: Northern
Electrical Services vs. The Environmentalists

This case functions partially as a consciousness-raising case. Thus, the case should begin with a thorough discussion of the questions for discussion. The case could be coordinated with a schoolwide Environmental Day, during which local business leaders, politicians, and environmentalists are brought to campus to discuss similar questions. Business students must be made aware of the seriousness of the situation as, too often, environmental concerns are not part of a business school curriculum.

The case itself provides an opportunity for a lively debate, and presentations often show a good deal of student creativity. For example, one group of environmentalists even brought in dead fish, which they claimed were found floating belly-up in the Connecticut River. On the more serious side, you must encourage the environmentalists to present their facts with statistics and charts. They must prove their case, as most of the members of the town meeting will be on the side of Northern Electrical Services due to a fear of unemployment. The environmentalists have to prove conclusively the health danger represented by Northern Electrical Services.

You must also see that the Northern Electrical Services team has prepared their case. One of their speakers should emphasize what their company is doing for the town both economically and socially. Have the speaker give a list of local programs that the company has supported. One of the speakers should be the company's environmental expert and should present studies showing that their emissions are within EPA (Environmental Protection Agency) standards. A third speaker could outline the impact on the town if Northern Electrical Services were forced to close their plant. This information should be presented factually, but not aggressively.

Students should have no trouble in preparing, but it doesn't hurt to "push" them a little. Make sure that all the groups prepare adequately. As this is an open meeting, some groups have a tendency to want to let the other groups do all the talking. Tell the class in advance that all groups will have to be active in the meeting.

The charge that Northern Electrical Services is responsible for dumping PCBs in the Connecticut River is a difficult accusation to prove. However, if the environmentalists have found a hidden pipe from the factory that could have drained waste water containing PCBs directly into the river, and if the area around the factory has high concentrations of PCBs, they would have a strong case. You must decide whether you want to suggest this possibility to the environmentalists. Finally, you must impress upon the representatives of the State Department of Environmental Protection the importance of being impartial.

CASE GOALS

1. Consciousness-raising about business people's environmental responsibilities and the trade-offs between the necessary expenses to clean up the environment and the social benefits of a clean environment.
2. Language skills necessary to present an opinion, to get others' opinions, and to disagree.
3. Argumentation skills. Use the worksheet in the Instructors' Manual from the "Other People's Money" case (page 13) and have each group fill it out.
4. Presentation skills for the groups representing Northern Electrical Services and the environmentalists, who should fill in the worksheets below. The other workers and local residents should balance health issues and possible loss of jobs in preparing their case.

WORKSHEET FOR THE MANAGEMENT OF NORTHERN ELECTRICAL SERVICES

Fill in the following sections:

1. What has your company done economically for the community in terms of jobs? What would happen to the town if you closed the factory?
2. What has your company done to support the community in other ways (for example, youth sports programs, cultural events, etc.)?
3. What has your company done to clean up the environment?
4. What is your company willing to do to protect the environment in the future?
5. Anticipate three arguments that you think the environmentalists will use and fill out the following counterargument worksheet:

Anticipated argument used by environmentalists:

Your counterargument:

Support for your position:

WORKSHEET FOR THE ENVIRONMENTALISTS

1. Compare the incidence of conditions such as respiratory illnesses, cancer, spontaneous abortions, and nausea in the local area with the national average. The local figures are provided in the case, and you should research national figures for the country where you presently reside or for the United States.

2. Compare emission rates of PCBs, sulfur dioxide, and nitrogen oxide for the factory with EPA limits. If your "tests" show that there are higher emissions than the 1.2 pounds per million BTUs of sulfur dioxide and 0.6 pounds per million BTUs of nitrogen dioxide claimed by Northern Electrical Services, state the amounts that you found.

3. Make a list of demands to Northern Electrical Services to clean up the local environment.

4. State how these demands, if carried out, will improve life in the local community.

5. Anticipate three arguments that you think the management of Northern Electrical Services will use and fill out the following counterargument worksheet:

Anticipated argument used by management:

Your counterargument:

Support for your position:

CLASS SESSIONS

First hour: Discussion questions. Choose/assign roles. Begin preparation of the groups' roles including the filling in of worksheets. Language feedback.

Second hour: Do the verbal exercise described in the Language Mastery section. Preparation for the meeting. Language feedback.

Third hour: Hold the meeting.

Fourth hour: Content and language feedback for the third and fourth hours.

NECESSARY BACKGROUND INFORMATION The information in this case is adequate to solve the case, but it could be supplemented by a guest lecturer from a local environmental organization or a professor or graduate student in environmental studies.

WORK EXPERIENCE: QUESTIONS FOR STUDENTS

What environmental problems are you facing in your country? What kinds of confrontations occur between various interests (business, environmentalist groups/Green Parties, government) when discussing the environment? Is there cooperation or confrontation? Explain why. Have you ever been involved in an environmental issue? Describe your experience, including your company's attitude toward demands for change or your personal experience as a participant.

CASE 7/Business Organization and Management: COMMUTAIR: Employee Motivation and Management Theory

Although motivation is a key issue in management, your students may not have studied it in detail. Thus, you may have to encourage them to read articles and chapters from organizational behavior and management texts and even provide them with articles on the subject. You might begin by discussing cultural attitudes toward work and the importance/necessity of having a motivational scheme in a company. You will probably find a wide range of attitudes, which can form the basis of an interesting discussion. A second issue might be the question of whether human resources departments in the students' countries consider motivational schemes important. Then you can discuss the nature of the Commutair employees' work and how that might influence what it takes to motivate them. Different work groups (for example, assembly workers, engineers, front-line employees in Commutair) will be motivated by different things. Is salary a stronger motivation than autonomy (having the power and delegated responsibility to make decisions that affect your job)? How important is job rotation?

Finally, you can discuss Commutair's present organizational chart and the problems in communication it might cause. Included on page 27 of this manual is a suggestion for a new organizational chart that is flatter and thus gives better opportunities for communication. Do not show this chart to the students. Let them work out their own organizational chart. After the above discussions, the students should be prepared to solve the case in groups.

CASE GOALS

1.   To consider the question of motivating employees.

2.   To develop analytical and problem-solving skills.

3.   To develop diplomatic language that reflects a positive attitude toward solving problems.

WORKSHEETS The following worksheets should be filled out by students in advance of the meeting.

Management

1. A managerial policy statement concerning management's attitude toward its employees.
2. A statement of a customer- and service-oriented policy expected to be followed by all levels of employees.

The front-line workers

1. A description of aspects of their present working situation that are unsatisfactory (for example, management's failure to respond to customer complaints and suggestions from employees).
2. A statement of what changes they would like to see implemented to solve the present problems in their work situation (for example, initiating a company policy that all suggestions from employees must be responded to within thirty days). Have the students use the diplomatic language from the Language Mastery exercise to give a positive tone to their statements.
3. A statement of the impact of these changes on motivation and performance (for example, greater employee satisfaction due to a feeling of control over the work situation and less frustration--both of which will lead to better customer service).

CLASS SESSIONS

First hour: Discussion questions. Choose/assign roles (such as human rescources department representative, check-in employee, etc.) The individual group members can begin filling out the above worksheet in preparation for the second hour. Language feedback.

Second hour: Review the assignment from the Language Mastery exercise. Continue preparing the four items for the oral/written report with an emphasis on the motivational package and a possible new organizational structure. The front-line employees will use their worksheets to present their suggestions, and the representative from the human resources department will present his or her worksheet for comments and suggestions from the front-line employees. Language feedback.

Third hour: Presentation of the four items. Each group can be assigned to present one of the items or one or two groups can present all of the items, followed by a discussion in which the other groups compare and contrast their solutions with those presented.

Fourth hour: Language and content feedback for the third and fourth hours.

NECESSARY BACKGROUND INFORMATION No additional information should be necessary to solve this case.

WORK EXPERIENCE: QUESTIONS FOR STUDENTS Have you ever been involved in a service sector company that has gone through the process of developing and implementing a new motivational strategy? If so, explain the process. Who initiated the process, the employees or the management? What problems did you face and how did you solve them? What did the motivational package consist of? How did the new strategy improve the working conditions and general atmosphere? How did the new strategy improve the employees' and the company's performance?

REVISED ORGANIZATIONAL CHART FOR COMMUTAIR The chart on page 27 illustrates a flatter organizational structure that should be more responsive to employees' questions and requests. The check-in, reservation, and baggage handling staff would report to the flight and reservations managers, who could confer with the appropriate person at the next level (general managers in Reservations, In-flight Operations, or Ground Operations). The general manager level would have direct access to the president if the need were to arise, and naturally the managing officers would have direct access to the President. The president would have an open-door policy to encourage responses from all levels.

CASE 8/Business Organization and Management: Unhealthy Leaders: Sterling Forklift

Like the previous case, this one deals with both employee relations and organizational structure. The new element here is the resistance to change by the president. The key to this case is Masters, and you should work closely with the students who are playing Masters during their preparation. They should enter the case determined to maintain the same hub and spoke organizational structure that places them at the center of all decision making. However, they must be told to be reasonable. If the other members of the meeting present a convincing argument, they must be willing to make concessions for the sake of the company.

This case carries the Commutair case's themes of motivation, decentralized responsibility, and problems of communication one step further as it involves personalities. Thus, students must be encouraged to "get into their roles" just like actors have to do. By this time, they should be familiar enough with role playing to take the next step into acting. However, you must

25

make them aware of the necessity of "getting into their roles," attempting to portray real live people. This case is also intended to help students crystallize in their minds what characterizes a positive leadership style.

Suggest to students portraying Dickerson and McNulty that they analyze the profit and loss statement for 199_. (Figure 8.2) They should note that both the return on sales percentage (5 percent) and market share (4.5 percent) are low. Return on sales usually runs around 7 to 10 percent and there is certainly room for improvement concerning market share. They could argue in favor of implementing an assembly line in that reducing production time by 20 percent would cut costs, thus resulting in a higher return on sales percentage. Another suggestion they could make is to take some of the savings from reduced production costs and cut prices to increase market share. A balance could be achieved by taking part of the savings in the form of increased return on sales and part in increased market share through cutting prices.

CASE GOALS

1.	To develop diplomatic language.

2.	To develop interpersonal and argumentation skills.

3.	To make students aware of positive and negative managerial styles.

ARGUMENTATION EXERCISE WORKSHEET Find three arguments for your point of view and then support them with facts or logic.

Example *Statement* (Dickerson to Masters): Establishing an assembly line will meet your two main criteria, cost efficiency and better quality control.

Support: It will reduce production costs by 20 percent and considerably reduce errors in production. (Dickerson might then refer to other factories which have implemented similar systems.)

COUNTERARGUMENTATION EXERCISE WORKSHEET Anticipate three arguments your opponents might use and then find counterarguments and support.

Example *Anticipated argument:* Masters is against assembly line production because of the initial costs and the fact that the factory will have to be closed down, which will create problems in supplying customers.

Counterargument: The saving in production will pay for the cost of the new assembly line, and the more efficient system will reduce errors in production.

REVISED ORGANIZATIONAL CHART FOR COMMUTAIR

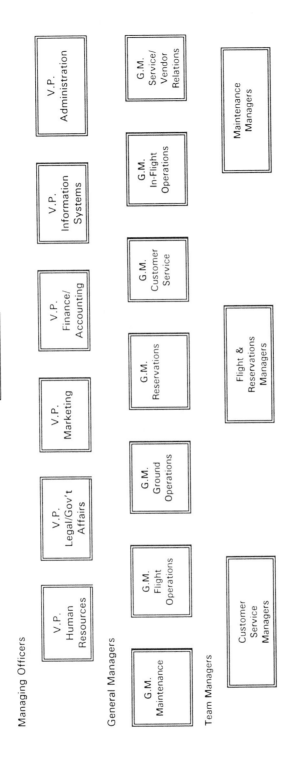

Managing Officers

President/ CEO

V.P. Human Resources

V.P. Legal/Gov't Affairs

V.P. Marketing

V.P. Finance/ Accounting

V.P. Information Systems

V.P. Administration

General Managers

G.M. Maintenance

G.M. Flight Operations

G.M. Ground Operations

G.M. Reservations

G.M. Customer Service

G.M. In-Flight Operations

G.M. Service/ Vendor Relations

Team Managers

Customer Service Managers

Flight & Reservations Managers

Maintenance Managers

In addition, problems of delivery due to the temporary closing of the factory can be avoided.

Support: A 20 percent reduction in production costs will allow Sterling Forklift to be more competitive by reducing prices and allowing expanded production. The payback period for the investment will be only three years. The workforce can work overtime in advance of the conversion to build up inventories and avoid delivery problems.

CLASS SESSIONS

First hour: Discussion questions. Choose/assign roles.
Each student will choose/be assigned a person to play (Masters, Dickerson, etc.) Fill out the worksheet above. Language feedback. If there is not time in class, have students fill out the worksheet as homework for the third session.

Second hour: Phase 1 as described in the case. Have the students playing Masters prepare together, establishing a feeling for what is going to happen in the meeting and how they intend to respond to suggestions by the other members. The students playing Dickerson will prepare separately, as will the students playing McNulty, McRoberts, and Smith. The individual preparation will be along lines established in the case concerning these characters' roles in the meeting. Thus, the students playing McRoberts should go over meeting vocabulary presented in the Case 3, "Other People's Money," and prepare a brief introduction about the team approach involving members of both Engineering and Production. The students playing McNulty and Smith should prepare details about how the team approach will work. They should also prepare drawings of an assembly line and an explanation of how it will be more cost-efficient and reduce errors in production. The students playing Dickerson should prepare a brief introduction of item two, the assembly line, and then a sentence to introduce McNulty and Smith who will give details. Language feedback.

Third hour: Phase 2 as described in the case, where students playing McRoberts, McNulty, Smith, and Dickerson meet to prepare (a) their solutions to the problems in cooperation, and with the assembly line, (b) their arguments in favor of these two items based on their worksheets, and (c) a strategy for the meeting with Masters. They should practice the Language Mastery exercises for this case and Case 7, "Commutair," as these exercises will help them to phrase their suggestions in a diplomatic manner. The students playing Masters will continue their preparation based on their expectations for the meeting. Language feedback.

Fourth hour: The meeting. You will have four to six meetings running concurrently depending on the number of students in your class.

Fifth hour: A presentation from two groups selected at random on the results of their meeting and how the results will influence the working environment at Sterling Forklift in the future. Language and content feedback. You can do language feedback after each session if time permits, or note the mistakes and comments and do everything in this last session. Language and content feedback for the fourth and fifth hours.

NECESSARY BACKGROUND INFORMATION No additional information should be necessary to solve this case.

WORK EXPERIENCE: QUESTIONS FOR STUDENTS

1. Have you ever had a boss who created a negative atmosphere on the job? What did he or she do to create this atmosphere, and what did employees do to deal with the problem?
2. What characterizes an "unhealthy leader," that is, a leader whose style leads to stress, illness, and a generally negative atmosphere?

(These questions are similar to those in the case, but they are designed to elicit personal experience).

CASE 9/Banking: Smith Brothers and Florida Central

This is a case for accountants and future bankers. Consider its use carefully and be sure that your students have an adequate background to solve it. It provides them with an opportunity to use banking vocabulary in a negotiation case. Due to the technical nature of this case, not only the information to understand the case, but also a solution have been provided here. However, do not provide students with a "canned" solution. You may use the information here to pose questions to the loan officers during their preparation. For example, (a) What do you think of the increase in receivables and inventories?; (b) How do you feel about their refusal to sign a personal guarantee?; and (c) What about Smith Brothers' activity (the relations between a company's current assets and its current liabilities, which help to determine the company's solvency, that is, its ability to pay its debts when due) and liquidity ratios?

Three significant issues need to be addressed before any formal lending agreement can be entered into. First, do we understand the credit as it is presented in the application? Second, how should the credit agreement be structured and priced if the loan request is granted? Third, who really is or should be in charge of establishing the terms of the agreement?

For the most part, Smith Brothers Building Materials appears to be an excellent credit risk for any bank. Several components of their loan application, however, would raise the red flag for any lender. Their increases in receivables and inventories raise questions about their credit policies, forecasting, purchasing, and general business activities. A loan officer would want to examine and explore the underlying reasons for these changes in their financial and operating position.

In addition, Zachary's reluctance to sign a personal guarantee would present a problem for many lending institutions. Although the bank would like to secure the family's business, would it really be worth it for them to sacrifice their own well-being to secure this business? The lenders would have to determine whether or not Zachary's refusal to sign a personal guarantee is enough to make them want to withdraw from any deal. The lender would also have to make a determination about the other terms presented by the borrower in his loan application. Would the stated interest rate provide the bank with a large enough return? Is granting the company unrestricted use of the funds too much of a risk? Would the bank be better off if it asserted more control over the business practices of the company if the loan were extended? Should the bank require that Smith Brothers provide some sort of collateral to secure the loan?

The bankers must also determine whether or not they want to allow Smith Brothers to exert so much control over the negotiation process. What would happen in the future if some problem arose and the loan were at risk? Would the bank be able to step in and assert the control necessary to safeguard their investment? Related to this issue are the multiple banking relationships Smith Brothers hopes to maintain. Does the creditor have to allow this and how should they feel about it?

SOLUTION Obviously, it is imperative to address the issues discussed above because they can have serious implications for the lender. A number of factors work in favor of approving the applicant's loan request. The management of the company is considered excellent and the company has been in business for a number of years.

The company's balance sheet is very strong, and the company continues to operate profitably. Its liquidity and activity ratios are excellent. The current ratio of 3.57 (7,028,244/1,971,000 = 3.57) indicates that the current assets are 3.57 times greater than the current liabilities. The acid test ratio (2,312,244/1,971,000 = 1.17), which measures liquidity in terms of cash, marketable securities, and receivables, also indicates that the company should be very capable of satisfying current operating needs. The liquidity position is excellent, so the company's ability to repay the line of credit is not a major issue.

Because of the vast family holdings, the bank could stand to gain substantial corporate and personal accounts from this relationship. Additionally, any trust or investment services provided for the family would generate fee income for the bank.

The company's facilities are located in booming areas. Florida has experienced significant growth over the past decade and many predict that this current building boom will last for another decade. The wide range of products sold by Smith Brothers should allow them to compete for sales in all construction markets.

The company's increased accounts receivable and inventories raise some concern. The increases have been rather dramatic, and the reasons for this must be discovered before the line of credit is granted. This situation may not be a problem now, but it could be an indication of future problems. The lack of significant long-term debt, however, also strengthens the applicant's position.

A consultant hired to analyze this case stated that she would probably grant the loan after examining some areas of the organization's operation. The credit terms requested by Zachary Smith, however, are far too liberal. She would require that the loan be secured with some form of collateral if Zachary refused to sign a personal guarantee. The proposed interest rate is far too low and wouldn't provide the bank with an adequate return on its investment. Perhaps the prime rate plus 2 percent would be agreeable to both parties. She would also request, because of Zachary's intent to maintain several banking relationships, that Smith Brothers maintain a minimum compensating balance at the bank. In addition, she would like Zachary to provide more information about his plans for the use of the funds. Is he planning to pay off old payables, purchase new inventories, or initiate a plan to foster growth? The financial statements prepared from the company's records should also be examined carefully. The bank could feel much more comfortable with this information if it were audited.

The company's operating profit (gross profit less operating expenses) dropped from $340,000 to $141,000, while other income increased by $147,000 during the same period. Where is the other income coming from? This indicates that a thorough examination of the subsidiaries is warranted because they represent a significant portion of the company's worth.

WORKSHEET FOR SMITH BROTHERS Have the students playing the roles of the Smith Brothers fill in answers for the following questions:

1. Why has your company suddenly increased its accounts receivable and inventories? For us they raise questions about your credit policies, sales forecasting, purchasing, and general business practices.
2. Why were assets shifted from cash to marketable equity securities in 1993? Has your cash management strategy changed?
3. Why do you refuse to sign a personal guarantee? A personal guarantee is considered common practice for this type of loan.
4. What do you intend to do with the loan proceeds?
5. You are requesting an interest rate of 0.3 percent above the prime rate, which is lower than that for any other loan we have granted. Why should we give you such a low rate?

CASE GOALS

1. To develop analytical, argumentation, and negotiation skills.
2. To develop banking vocabulary.
3. To practice informal meeting terminology.

CLASS SESSIONS

First hour: A detailed review of the discussion questions. Choose/assign roles. Language feedback.

Second hour: Preparation of roles. The loan officers should review the questions provided for their interview and be sure that they understand them. They should also prepare questions to test Smith Brothers' sound business sense. They should work out terms for the loan. Smith Brothers should develop a case in support of their loan application and the terms they are seeking and prepare answers to the loan officers' questions. They should fill in the above worksheet individually before class, and discuss their arguments and arrive at the best possible ones for the interview. Language feedback.

Third hour: The meeting between the loan officer and Smith Brothers.

Fourth hour: Presentation and discussion of the results of the meetings. Was the loan granted and on what terms? Language and content feedback for the third and fourth hours.

NECESSARY BACKGROUND INFORMATION The information to help solve this case is presented above and can be given to the students to the degree necessary.

WORK EXPERIENCE: QUESTIONS FOR STUDENTS Have you ever been interviewed in connection with either a personal or commercial loan application? What questions were asked, and what did the banker seem to consider most important? Describe the interview.

OPEN-ENDED CASES

The remaining cases are open-ended, which means that the students must (1) obtain the information to solve them from the local area, and (2) discuss and develop information-gathering strategies. These cases are unique because (a) they are as realistic as possible, being set in a real situation, (b) they take the case solving out of the classroom, and (c) they help students develop vital information-gathering skills. To help students make the transition from the closed-ended cases (where the material necessary to solve them is in the book and/or suggested bibliographic material), it is important to begin each open-ended case with a discussion of where to obtain the necessary material. In addition, the students may need more reference material, depending on their knowledge of the case's field. Student "experts" can be appointed to make background presentations, or experts can be brought in from outside if necessary. For example, in the marketing cases, a student or group could make a presentation about the 4 Ps (product, price, place, and promotion) leading a discussion and a question and answer period.

These cases should generally follow the sequence of discussion, case introduction, case preparation, case presentation, and language/content feedback used in the closed-ended cases. An emphasis should be placed on information-gathering strategies, and each group that presents should discuss how and where they obtained their material. By the time the students have completed a couple of these cases, they should have a whole new attitude toward information gathering and problem solving. Worksheets for the open-ended cases are not provided. By this time, the students should be able to structure their own work, which is also a skill the case study method helps develop.

CASE 10/Marketing: Penetrating the Market with Long-range Golf Clubs and Bags

As stated above, all the remaining cases are open-ended. Thus we move to the next level, where students must provide their own information. Each case introduction should include a brainstorming session on where to obtain the necessary information to solve the case. We live in the age of information and access to information is one major key to success. It is important to impress this fact on the students and to encourage them to develop information-gathering skills and techniques. Once again, emphasize that this course is more than "just" an English or business communications course.

A second emphasis in Case 10 is group presentation skills. In the presentation, the group must function as a unit, but one person should act as an anchorperson who introduces the presentation and makes some concluding statements. This role can be assigned to one of the group members who either has no other role or plays another, smaller role (for example, discussing distribution channels, which is the easiest role in the case). As part of the introduction to the case, discuss what makes a good group presentation. Aspects to be covered include the following:

1. A clear introduction setting out the segments of the presentation.
2. A clear conclusion summarizing the presentation.
3. A smooth transition between speakers, including an introduction of the next speaker and his or her topic. For example:
> Eva: "Now Bob will tell us about our distribution channels."
> Bob: "Thank you Eva. As Eva said, I will present our plan of distribution."

33

4.   Professional visual aids to illustrate your points. These should be in the form of overheads, flip charts, slides, or videos. *Creativity* and *clarity* should be the key words here.

All the groups are potential presenters and must go through the preparations. However, choose only two of the groups at random to present. After choosing them, give them a day or two to polish their presentations. After each presentation, have the class critique their performance based on criteria such as those mentioned above and any others that you might add. Emphasize the group presentation techniques presented in the Language Mastery Exercise. Groups that are not chosen this time should be asked to present in subsequent cases.

CASE GOALS

1.   To develop brainstorming as a creative solution device. In brainstorming, all suggestions, no matter how radical they seem, are accepted and written down. This allows for freedom of thought. The suggestions are later critically analyzed and either accepted or rejected.
2.   To develop group presentation skills.
3.   To practice marketing vocabulary
4.   To practice using transitional expressions.

CLASS SESSIONS

First hour: A discussion of information-gathering techniques.   An introduction to the 4 Ps, market analysis, segmentation, target group selection, and positioning.   Assign these introductions to various groups that will be responsible for the information and the question and answer period afterward. Language feedback.

Second hour: A continuation of the presentations mentioned above. Group work in which each group starts discussing the various aspects of the project and divides the tasks among the group members. Language feedback.

Third hour: Group members report back to the group about the information they have obtained, and the group starts to prepare their presentation. Language feedback.

Fourth hour: The same as in the third session. Two preparation sessions should be adequate, but be prepared to extend the preparation time to a third session if necessary. Language feedback.

Fifth hour: Presentation by two of the groups.

Sixth hour: A discussion of the information-gathering strategies used by the students.   Language and content feedback for the fifth and sixth hours. Emphasize group presentation skills and critique the presentation style of the two groups.

NECESSARY BACKGROUND INFORMATION A standard marketing textbook covers the idea of the 4 Ps. If the class does not know much about marketing, assign a presentation of the 4 Ps to a group (preferably a group made up of marketing students, which you can draw from all of the groups).

WORK EXPERIENCE: QUESTIONS FOR STUDENTS Have you ever been involved in a marketing campaign? Describe the elements of the campaign with which you were involved, such as market segmentation, product profiling, product distribution, advertising campaign, and so on.

CASE 11/Marketing: Costa de los Años de Oro

This case further develops the skills introduced in Case 10, on Marketing Long-range Golf Equipment. These cases are placed consecutively to reinforce the marketing concepts. As in the Long-range case, students should brainstorm about sources of information and discuss group presentation techniques. One of the goals of this course is to help students become independent and confident presenters. Progress toward this goal should be evident by now, and little time should be necessary in teaching and reinforcing these skills. However, remember that it is important to give positive feedback when signs that students have learned the intended skills become apparent, as reinforcement is an excellent motivational tool.

CASE GOALS

1. To develop brainstorming as a creative solution device. In brainstorming, all suggestions, no matter how radical they seem, are accepted and written down. This allows for freedom of thought. The suggestions are later critically analyzed and either accepted or rejected.
2. To develop group presentation skills.
3. To practice marketing vocabulary.
4. To practice social English.

CLASS SESSIONS

First hour: A discussion of information-gathering techniques. An introduction to market analysis, segmentation, target group selection, and positioning. Assign these topics to various groups, which will be responsible for the information and question and answer period afterward. Language feedback.

Second hour: A continuation of the presentations mentioned above. Group work in which each group starts discussing the various aspects of the project and divides the tasks among the group members. Language feedback.

Third hour: Group members report back to the group about the information they have obtained, and the group starts to prepare their presentation. Language feedback.

Fourth hour: The same as in the third session. Two preparation sessions should be adequate, but be prepared to extend the preparation time to a third session if necessary. Language feedback.

Fifth hour: Presentation by two of the groups.

Sixth hour: A discussion of the information-gathering strategies used by the students. Language and content feedback for the fifth and sixth hours. Emphasize group presentation skills and critique the presentation style of the two groups.

NECESSARY BACKGROUND INFORMATION See Case 10, "Penetrating the Market with Long-range Clubs and Bags."

WORK EXPERIENCE: QUESTIONS FOR STUDENTS Again, see Case 10, "Penetrating the Market with Long-range Golf Clubs and Bags."

CASE 12/Environment: Industrial Pollution: Charting Pollution and Proposing Solutions

This case brings the ideas presented in Case 6, "Northern Electrical Services vs. the Environmentalists," close to home. The problem is made realistic as the students are forced to confront it in their own "backyard." Dealing with environmental groups and companies in this case should help students see the full scope of the problem. This is a touchy issue, and the students will have to be diplomatic, particularly in dealing with the companies involved. No company likes to have their environmental "sins" made public. However, if they are not dealt with, environmental conditions will only continue to deteriorate.

The presentation in this case is much like the confrontation between management and the environmentalists in Case 6, and students should be able to play it without much help. They should have arrived at a level of competence where they require very little prompting.

CASE GOALS

1. Develop group presentation technique.
2. Practice appropriate tone and make the students aware of word choice to create the intended tone.
3. Reinforce the awareness of environmental issues introduced in "Northern Electrical Services vs. the Environmentalists."
4. Develop investigative and critical-analytical skills.

36

CLASS SESSIONS

First hour: A discussion of information gathering techniques and strategies and the discussion questions. Selection of a company to target. Choose/assign roles (the environmentalists and management). Language feedback.

Second hour: Group work in which each group starts discussing the various aspects of the project and divides the tasks among the group members. Language feedback.

Third hour: Group members report back to the group about the information they have obtained, and the group starts to prepare their presentation. Language feedback.

Fourth hour: The same as in the third session. Two preparation sessions should be adequate, but be prepared to extend the preparation time to a third session if necessary. Language feedback.

Fifth hour: Presentation in which one of the environmental groups is chosen to present their findings and one of the management groups is chosen to defend the company. Try to get the environmentalists and management to come to some form of a compromise agreement.

Sixth hour: A discussion of the information-gathering strategies used by students. Language and content feedback for the fifth and sixth hours. Emphasize group presentation skills and critique the presentation style of the two groups.

NECESSARY BACKGROUND INFORMATION See Case 6, "Northern Electrical Services vs. The Environmentalists"

WORK EXPERIENCE: QUESTIONS FOR STUDENTS Again, see Case 6, "Northern Electrical Services vs. the Environmentalists."

CASE 13/International Trade: Competing Internationally

The presentation of this case is clearly defined in the case description. The major problem in this case is knowledge. Ideally, your students will have completed a course in business organization and management or even better, in competitive management. However, if not, they can obtain the necessary information in the sources cited. This case or Case 14 can serve as a "final exam," as both are fairly complicated. If you are going to use one of them as a final exam, you might ask the students which one they prefer. By now, the students should be on their own. The book begins with highly structured cases and gradually the cases become less structured as students develop the skills to provide the structure themselves. We have now arrived at the final stage of the course, at which point students should be able to prepare and present their findings with a minimum of help.

CASE GOALS

1.   To develop comparative skills and the language to express comparisons.
2.   To develop critical-analytical and strategic planning skills.
3.   To develop group presentation techniques.

CLASS SESSIONS

First hour: A discussion of information-gathering skills and the various aspects of competitive analysis. It might be necessary to bring in outside expertise if your students lack knowledge in this area. Selection of the British company and competing companies in other countries. The teacher can make suggestions based on available literature.   Language feedback.

Second hour: Library session where students are familiarized with works on the subject. Students can begin reading and divide tasks.

Third hour: Group members report back to the group about the information they have obtained, and the group starts to prepare their presentation. Language feedback.

Fourth hour: The same as in the third session. Two preparation sessions should be adequate, but be prepared to extend the preparation time to a third session if necessary. Language feedback.

Fifth and sixth hours: Presentation of the British company in terms of some or all of the twelve items mentioned in the case, including production costs, product quality, research and development, etc. Presentation of the other companies. Take as many sessions as necessary to complete the case. Language feedback.

Seventh hour: Presentation of the British company's future strategy for competition, taking into account what has been learned about the competition. Language and content feedback.

NECESSARY BACKGROUND INFORMATION This case requires the information provided in the books recommended in the student text.

WORK EXPERIENCE: QUESTIONS FOR STUDENTS How you ever been part of a strategy-planning team to develop a plan to meet foreign competition? Describe the activities of this team.

CASE 14/Business Organization and Management: Saturn: Can American Automobile Manufacturers Compete with the Japanese?

As mentioned in the case, the report from this case could serve as a term paper for the course. The oral presentation could serve as a final presentation for a grade. This case and Case 13, "Competing Internationally," are the two most difficult cases in the book. If you are going to use one of them as a final exam, you might ask the students which one they prefer. Both will adequately test the skills that the students were expected to attain in using this book.

As stated in the suggestions for Case 13, "Competing Internationally", the students should primarily be left to their own resources for this case. However, a brainstorming session on where to get information would be helpful. In your preparation for the case, collect useful written material (articles, brochures from Saturn, etc.) so that you can give students hints on where to find such materials. However, let them try to find their own materials, and only give them your materials if absolutely necessary. You must strike a balance between encouraging the students to find their own material and preventing them from getting frustrated if enough material is not available.

CASE GOALS

1. To develop comparative skills and the language to express comparisons.
2. To develop critical-analytical and strategic planning skills.
3. To develop group presentation technique.

CLASS SESSIONS

First hour: A discussion of information-gathering skills and the beginning of group work in which each group member chooses one of the four areas: engineering, production, human resources, or organizational structure. Language feedback.

Second hour: Library session where students are familiarized with works on the subject. Students can begin reading and prepare for the discussion on various aspects of the case, such as engineering, production, human resources and organization.

Third hour: Discuss important aspects of the four areas such as:

1. *Engineering:* the importance of quality, durability and customer-responsive engineering (producing cars that people want, not just cars that companies want people to want).
2. *Production:* the use of robots and how to reduce production time. (This subject may be difficult, so you might want to concentrate primarily on the other three.)
3. *Human resources:* the Japanese life-long job security idea versus the

lack of job security in the United States. Discuss management's differing attitudes toward workers and the workers' differing attitudes toward work, the company, and management.

4.   *Organizational structure:* Discuss how differing organizational structures reflect different human resource policies and how these structures help or hinder quick responses to changing markets.

The students from each group assigned these areas will be expected to contribute to the discussion of their area. Language feedback.

Fourth hour: Phase 1 preparation (see case). Language feedback.
Fifth hour: Phase 2 task force meeting (see case). Language feedback.
Sixth hour: Presentation. Take as many sessions as is necessary depending on the length and number of presentations. All groups should present.
Seventh hour: Language and content feedback for the sixth hour.

NECESSARY BACKGROUND INFORMATION This case requires information provided in the sources mentioned in the student text.

WORK EXPERIENCE: QUESTIONS FOR STUDENTS Why do you think the Japanese have been so successful? What aspects of their total strategy would you recommend that your company adopt?

APPENDIX 1/TELEPHONE ENGLISH

As is mentioned in the exercise, mastering telephone English is extremely important because much business communication occurs by telephone. Let students practice in pairs until they feel comfortable with the exercises. Then have a pair do an exercise for the class, and have the class evaluate the performance along the lines suggested in the book, following the seven steps and being polite, informative, and customer-oriented. Do four or five pairs. Do this at two-week intervals throughout the semester to perfect students' skills. This is one skill that they absolutely must master, and periodic drill is important.

KEY FOR THE FILL-IN

Use the following key words and phrases for using the telephone to fill in the blanks in the sentences below.

to dial to transfer to connect you to be put on hold
to call back to page radio pager wrong number
information (British: directory inquiries)
local call long-distance call (British: trunk call)
operator switchboard telephone number extension

Operator: This is information /directory inquiries. What city, please?

Mr. Jones: Boston. The telephone number for A. J. Smiths.

Operator: Their number is 678-8897.

Mr. Jones: Is that a local or long-distance/trunk call from a 665 exchange?

Operator: It's in the same area so it's a local call.

Mr. Jones: Thank you, Operator.

Switchboard Operator at A. J. Smiths: A. J. Smith's. Good morning.

Mr. Jones: Mr. Johnson at extension 255, please.

Switchboard Operator: Just a moment, I'll connect you.

Mr. Williams: Accounting, Mr. Williams.

Mr. Jones: Excuse me. Is this extension 255?

Mr. Williams: No, I'm sorry. This is 253.

Mr. Jones: Oh, the switchboard operator connected me with the wrong number/extension.

Mr. Williams: No problem. I'll transfer your call to 255.

Mrs. Dickson: Mr. Johnson's telephone.

Mr. Jones: Is Mr. Johnson in?

Mrs. Dickson: No, he isn't, but I can page him. He has a radio pager. Oh excuse me. Mr. Johnson is in the next office. I can hear his voice, but he's on another line. Do you want me to put you on hold or do you want to call back later?

Mr. Smith: You can put me on hold.

APPENDIX 2/BUSINESS WRITING
WRITING STYLE AND TONE

The purpose of this section is to make the students' style more sophisticated. I suggest going through the examples of polite/diplomatic phrases and having students correct the ten sentences to make the phrasing more polite/diplomatic, then having the students complete the letter writing assignment to check that they have internalized these phrases and the necessity of using them. Remember, there is no one right answer to each of the ten sentences. The important thing is that the corrected sentence is more sophisticated.

St. Martin's Press